THE
RAYS
AND ESOTERIC
PSYCHOLOGY

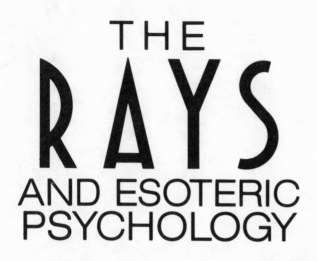

THE
RAYS
AND ESOTERIC PSYCHOLOGY

Zachary F. Lansdowne

SAMUEL WEISER, INC.
York Beach, Maine

First published in 1989 by
Samuel Weiser, Inc.
Box 612
York Beach, Maine 03910

Library of Congress Cataloging-in-Publication Data

Lansdowne, Zachary F.
    The rays and esoteric psychology.

    Bibliography: p.
    1. Seven rays (Occultism)   2. Bailey, Alice, 1880-1949.
Treatise on the seven rays.   3. Theosophy.   I. Title
BP573.S47L36 1989   299'.934   89-5547
ISBN 0-87728-682-5

Cover illustration ©1989 Michael Martin

Typeset in 11 point Baskerville
Printed in the United States of America by
McNaughton & Gunn, Inc.

Contents

List of Tables

Acknowledgments

Appreciation is expressed to the following individuals for their careful and thoughtful comments on an earlier version of this book: Elizabeth Douphner, Alicia Hinkle, and Tony Townsend. Appreciation is also expressed to the Lucis Publishing Company for permission to quote from the several books by Alice A. Bailey.

Introduction

The various schools of modern psychology have gathered much information about how we function, including our complexes, psychoses, neuroses, and instincts. Also revealed are the relationships between our behavior and our nervous system, brain, and endocrine glands. However, modern psychology is somewhat limited and circumscribed for several reasons. Clinical psychology tends to focus on studying abnormal or pathological individuals, rather than normal people. Experimental psychology tends to be external in its orientation, in the sense that it focuses on a person's behavior rather than the indwelling self. While some schools of psychology do acknowledge that there is a self, or a principle that informs the physical body and expresses its reactions through various emotional and mental states, there is much confusion about the nature of that self. Is the self separate and detached from the physical body? Is it just a mental image or a thought? Or is the self the aggregated life and consciousness of the physical cells?

In contrast, *esoteric* psychology is primarily concerned with the soul, or self, which is the ensouling entity or integrating principle within the physical form. According to esoteric psychology, as understood by various theosophical writers, a human being consists of a personality, a soul, and a spirit. The personality has four aspects: the concrete mind, or mental body, which gives the power of discrimination; the emotional body, which gives the capacity to sense, desire, aspire, and attract; the vital or energy body, which gives the power to act and be energetic; and the dense physical body, which is controlled by the three preceding aspects and enables activity to take place in the physical world. The soul has two aspects: intuition and will, or purpose. The informing, indwelling soul seeks to impress, impel, and motivate the personality. The personality and soul are in turn animated and impelled by the spirit, which is the energy of life itself. These various aspects of the human being become integrated over time in a gradual and progressive manner. This book focuses on the process in which the personality becomes integrated with and dominated by the soul.

In esoteric psychology, a *ray* is defined as a particular quality of energy. It is said that there are seven different rays or qualities of energy, and the soul, or self, of a human being is expressive of one or another of the seven rays. Consequently, the seven rays provide a typology, a way of classifying human beings in terms of the essential qualities of their souls.

H. P. Blavatsky, the founder of the Theosophical Society, published in 1888 the first known use of the phrase "seven rays" in the following passage from *The Secret Doctrine*: "There are seven chief groups of . . . Dhyan Chohans, which groups will be found and recognized in every religion, for they are the primeval Seven Rays. Humanity, occultism teaches us, is divided into seven distinct groups."[1] In this quotation, the phrase *Dhyan Chohans* is a Sanskrit-Tibetan compound expression meaning "Lords of Meditation," and it can be interpreted as referring to the souls of human beings.

Later, other theosophical writers, such as E. Wood[2] and G. Hodson,[3] compiled material regarding the seven rays, and A. A. Bailey wrote an extensive five-volume treatise on the subject.[4] More recently, several authors have provided general surveys on the teachings of the seven rays,[5] applied these teachings within the school of psychology known as psychosynthesis,[6] and also applied them within various systems of healing.[7] There is now even a scholarly journal dedicated to studying the seven rays and their various applications.[8]

The fundamental premise of this book is that the soul of each human being is expressive of one of the seven rays. Through its quality, the ray of the soul affects the nature of the mental, emotional, vital, and dense physical bodies; predisposes us to certain strengths and weaknesses; and influences how we relate to other human beings. As we evolve along the spiritual path, our ray determines our destiny in the sense that it predisposes us toward certain activities.

How an individual's soul becomes integrated with and dominates the personality depends on the soul's ray. Alice A. Bailey published a "Technique of Integration" for each of the seven rays, describing this process. However, as Bailey herself pointed out, her "study of the Techniques of Integration was definitely abstruse and couched in language quite symbolic."[9] The purpose of this book is to interpret and clarify these symbolic techniques.

In the commentary to be given on the Technique of Integration for each ray, the following four phases of the spiritual path are discussed:

1. The point of crisis that marks the beginning of what is called the path of probation.

2. The path of probation itself, during which we become aware of higher values and begin to reorient our lives, culminating in what is called the first initiation.

3. The path of discipleship between the first and second initiations, during which we purify our emotional nature.

4. The path of discipleship between the second and third initiations, during which the personality and soul begin to fuse *in*

consciousness with various physiological and psychological effects.

Why is studying these Techniques of Integration important? Within the consciousness of every human being is a sense of duality. In some mysterious sense, each person is two beings, and it is the warfare between the two that leads to the various neuroses and complexes. The Apostle Paul referred to this warfare when he said: "For what I would, that do I not; but what I hate, that do I" (Rom. 7:15). By understanding the Techniques of Integration, it is possible to comprehend better the nature of these warring forces, how these forces can be integrated, and how this process of integration varies among the seven rays.

There is an important relationship between the Techniques of Integration and yoga. The Sanskrit word *yoga* is sometimes used to signify the concept of union: such as the union of a human being with God, the mortal with the eternal, or the mind with the innermost center of one's own being. This word is also used to denote a system of self-development the observance of which can lead to union. Thus, the word *yoga* can refer either to the goal of union or the path leading to that goal. A fundamental concept, discussed in textbooks on yoga, is that people belong to different psychological types. A number of different systems of yoga have been devised, with each system being a line of self-development for a particular psychological type. Another fundamental concept is that of freedom in spiritual investigation, so that one can find the system of yoga that is most appropriate for one's own psychological make-up.[10]

It is shown in this book that the typology of the seven rays can be used to relate systems of yoga to psychological types. In particular, it is shown that there is an organized system of thought, such as a traditional system of yoga, similar to the Technique of Integration for each ray. Consequently, a comprehensive philosophy of yoga can be formulated with the aid of the seven rays and Bailey's symbolic techniques.

It might be asked: Why did Bailey write these techniques in such a disguised way? If these techniques are so important, why were they not written so that they could be easily understood? While much of Bailey's work is straightforward and easy to read, from time to time she placed in her volumes certain symbolic passages that are quite abstruse, and the Techniques of Integration are one such instance. The presence of these symbolic passages makes her books unique and distinctive, and there are several explanations for their inclusion. One explanation is that a potent way of drawing the intuition into activity is through the study and interpretation of symbols. According to Bailey, the study of symbols will produce three effects when pursued faithfully and diligently: it develops the power to penetrate behind the form and arrive at the subjective reality; it helps to establish a close alignment among the brain, mind, and soul; and it arouses into activity certain unawakened areas of the brain.[11]

Bailey had a second reason for including symbolic passages in her books. To some extent she wrote for the future and used symbols to ensure that the deeper aspects of her teaching would emerge only after proper preparation and readiness were present. She considered her readers as a channel through which a particular facet of the Ageless Wisdom would reach the waiting world, and she called on her readers to comprehend intuitively and to adapt her material. Bailey predicted that certain of her symbolic passages would eventually be interpreted and clarified by other writers, resulting in the appearance of a future teaching that would utilize her books as a background. Concerning her material on the seven rays, she wrote the following in 1934: "Learn to grasp the teaching correctly, and see it for what it is. Some of it is written for a distant time, and the true significance of this *Treatise on the Seven Rays* will begin to emerge as part of the general knowledge of humanity only towards the close of this century."[12]

Chapter 1 discusses the basic characteristics for each of the seven rays. Chapter 2 gives an interpretation and explanation of Bailey's Technique of Integration for each ray. And chapter 3 demonstrates the practicality and usefulness of these ideas by applying them to the following areas: psychotherapy, ray analysis, subjective guidance, self-observation, character building, emotional purification, and service.

Chapter 1

The Seven Rays

A human being is sentient and self-conscious and can become group conscious. It is important to distinguish between these terms. Sentiency refers to the capacity of responding sensitively to contact with the environment. For instance, vegetables and animals are sentient. However, unlike vegetables and animals, a human being has the additional capacity of self-consciousness: the faculty whereby we become aware of being the indwelling self within the body, of being the one who is evolving by means of experiences, and of being different from other human beings. After the self-consciousness aspect is perfected, we can develop group consciousness. The latter is the same as inclusive love and is experienced as an intuitive perception of the essential unity of human beings.

The stages of evolution for a human being can be described as follows:

1. *Sensual*. Infants are vital sentient beings who are polarized in their physical bodies, without any aspirations except to experience the pleasures of the body and without any intelligent understanding of their environment.

2. *Emotional*. Children are generally polarized in the emotional body with an active wish-life and imagination. Their minds are beginning to be active, and they have desires that are not purely physical. Because their minds are not sufficiently developed to establish balance or equilibrium, children suffer from emotional extremes such as intense devotion and hatred.

3. *Mental*. Adolescents develop a mental consciousness that is intelligent, enquiring, and intellectually sensitive. However, their personalities are not yet coordinated, in the sense that their mental focus may alternate in emphasis with the earlier stages of emotionality and sensuality.

4. *Ambition*. Young adults develop a sense of responsibility to family members and feel important by regarding others as being dependent. They become ambitious and long for influence and power in some field of endeavor.

5. *Coordination*. Owing to ambition, average adults learn to coordinate the energies of personality, so that brain and mind function synchronously. The emotional nature is subordinated, and there is steady growth in the power to use thought.

6. *Selfish influence*. Because of their capacity to live a coordinated life, advanced adults attain the power to influence, sway, guide, and hold others within their range of purpose and desire. Since the higher issues are not yet understood, this power is selfishly used and is frequently destructive.

7. *Group awareness*. In this final stage, aspirants seek to be soul-centered and controlled. They steadily develop group consciousness, or inclusive love, while preserving their self-consciousness and sense of individuality.[1]

In stages one through five of the list above, the individuals are learning how to function as coordinated personalities. During these stages, they are preeminently self-centered, which is a necessary step on the way to higher consciousness. When the sixth stage is reached, their personalities are coordinated; their characteristics include dominance, ambition, pride, and lack of inclusive love, although they may possess love for those whom they feel are necessary for their comfort. During the seventh stage, they begin to express selflessness, group service, and inclusive love. In theosophical terminology, the seventh stage includes both the paths of probation and discipleship.

It is important to ascertain one's stage on the developmental ladder. For individuals in the first through fifth stages, a step forward is learning to express the energies of their personalities in a self-centered but coordinated way. For those at the sixth stage, a step forward is learning to experiment with their powers and gather around themselves people who look up to them, who feed their pride and ambition, and who make them influential and important. For those entering the seventh stage, a step forward is learning to relinquish self-centeredness and seeing things in a newer and truer perspective.

The focus of this book is on those who are leaving the sixth stage and are beginning to enter the seventh stage. Because the sixth stage has been reached, the mental, emotional, and physical energies of the personality have been successfully coordinated. As a result, such people have potent personalities and are at the center of some group or organization. They are influential magnetic persons who sway others and coordinate them into larger activities. They may be the head of a business, political party, religious body, or even a nation. However, a discontent gradually arises in them because the savor of their life experience begins to be unsatisfactory. Another shift in polarization starts to occur: at first unconsciously and later consciously, they reach out to the life and meaning of a faintly sensed inner reality. The soul is beginning to make its presence felt and to grip more actively the personality.

It is at this point that the information regarding the seven rays becomes valuable. The soul of each human being is to be found on one or another of the seven rays, and the soul's ray determines the manner in which the soul becomes integrated with the personality. Thus, there are seven different processes of integration, one for each ray. The soul is the integrating factor and applies the process of control and integration to the personality.

The characteristics for each of the seven rays are discussed in the remainder of this chapter. For each ray, a symbolic statement is given that was originally published by Bailey but without a detailed explanation. This statement describes the reactions of the corresponding ray type to incarnating in the material world and identifying with material form. Following the symbolic statement is a commentary that includes a discussion of the basic quality of the ray, the characteristic reactions during the stage of selfish influence, the crisis of evocation that marks the end of that stage, and the unfoldment needed during the stage of group awareness. According to Bailey, these seven symbolic statements, when properly understood, give "the keynote of the new psychology."[2]

It is important to emphasize that the interpretations given for Bailey's symbolic statements, both in this chapter and the next, are solely the responsibility of this writer and may not be what was originally intended. The reader must be the judge of the accuracy of the interpretations.

Ray One

The Blessed One flies like an arrow into matter. He destroys (or ruptures) the way by which he might return. He grounds himself deeply in the depths of form.

He asserts: "I will return. My power is great. I will destroy all obstacles. Nothing can stop my progress to my goal. Around me lies that which I have destroyed. What must I do?"

The answer comes: "Order from chaos, O Pilgrim on the way of death, this is the way for you. Love you must learn. Dynamic will you have. The right use of destruction for the furtherance of the Plan, must be the way for you. Adherence to the rhythm of the planet will release the hidden Blessed One and order bring."[3]

The first ray is called the ray of will or power. The basic quality for persons on this ray is dynamic purpose, and the basic technique is grasping what they need. Their will power is strong, for either good or evil. This power works out as strength, courage, and steadfastness, but it also works out as a destructive force with an apparent cruelty and impersonality. First-ray persons often have strong feelings and affections but do not readily express them. They are born leaders, generally found at the head of their professions. As soldiers, they would be able commanders-in-chief. They rarely are artists. As writers, their literary works would be strong and trenchant, with little regard for style and polish.[4]

It is important to distinguish between the mental body, which is the highest aspect of the personality, and the soul. The mental body deals with knowledge, particulars, or what are called concrete thoughts—for instance, a particular tree, car, or triangle. The mental body is the instrument for concrete thinking and expresses concrete thoughts through the physical brain. In contrast, the soul is concerned with principles or abstract thoughts: trees or cars in general or the principle of triangularity common to all triangles. The soul is the instrument for abstract thinking and is the storehouse for the abstracted essence, or wisdom, gained from experiences. Due to the presence of the soul, a human being is able to have self-consciousness and develop group consciousness.

In the symbolic statement given above, "the Blessed One" refers to an individual with a first-ray soul. The viewpoint here is that the soul exists prior to physical incarnation and then acquires a personality consisting of the mental, emotional, and physical bodies. The *involutionary* path consists of appropriating the personality energies, incarnating into the material world, engaging in activities with a personal or selfish intent, and then becoming engrossed with material living. The *evolutionary* or spiritual path consists of awakening from the thrall of material living, expressing the selflessness that is a major characteristic of the soul, emerging into the light of the soul, and then becoming centered in the kingdom of heaven. Thus, the spiritual path can be viewed as "the path of return," because it retraces the steps, albeit in the opposite direction, of the earlier involutionary path.[5] This same cycle is described in the Bible as the parable of the prodigal son (Luke 15:11–32).

The first paragraph in the symbolic statement given above corresponds to the stage of selfish influence, which is the last stage of the involutionary path. Through the use of soul powers, first-ray individuals have attained dynamic one-pointedness, enabling them to move forward and achieve their materialistic goals in an unalterable and undeviating way ("The Blessed One flies like an arrow into matter"). Their longing for power and authority prevents them from receiving the guidance of the soul, which would enable them to tread the path of return ("He destroys the way by which he might return"). By expressing their strength and self-will to dominate others, they engulf themselves in feelings of lovelessness and isolation ("He grounds himself deeply in the depths of form"). Due to this selfish use of power, they evoke a display of antagonistic power in response.

The key to understanding the first paragraph is recognizing this: It is possible to use some of the powers of the soul without being guided by the soul. To describe how the powers of the soul unfold over time, Bailey represents the soul in the form of a twelve-petaled lotus, called the egoic lotus. Each of the twelve petals symbolizes a specific power or capacity to use abstract thought. The unfoldment of a given petal occurs when we have abstracted the corresponding essence, or wisdom, from our various experiences. In particular, we are able to unfold or open three of these petals by the end of the stage of selfish influence, which is before we begin to be guided by the soul. Thus, we are able to use about one-fourth of the potential soul powers for the purposes of coordinating our personalities and achieving the separative ambitions of our personalities. The remaining petals, or powers, unfold during the subsequent evolutionary path.[6]

The second paragraph corresponds to the point where the involutionary path ends and the evolutionary path begins. After having unfolded some soul powers to achieve their materialistic ambitions, first-ray individuals are able to sense intuitively their basic divine nature. As a result, they no longer can remain satisfied with gaining power in a personality sense and begin to tread the path of return ("I will return"). This point in life is called the crisis of evocation, because they begin to evoke the guidance of the soul. Their characteristic method of treading the spiritual path is by sheer force of will: they sense the power that they have as first-ray souls ("My power is great"), are determined to overcome all impediments in their personalities ("I will destroy all obstacles"), and have confidence that nothing can stop their progress to their new goal of rendering true service ("Nothing can stop my progress to my goal"). The first step on this path is observing one's life from the vantage point of the soul and realizing that one has trampled on other human beings for self-centered purposes ("Around me lies that which I have destroyed"). The next step is evoking the wisdom of the soul to understand the changes that must be made in the personality ("What must I do?").

The third paragraph refers to the stage of group awareness, which is the first stage of the evolutionary path. Through intuitive answers that come from the soul, first-ray individuals are guided to establish "order from chaos." By using the first ray of will without love or wisdom, they created chaos ("O Pilgrim on the way of death"). They must now learn to create order through uniting these characteristics ("this is the way for you"). Thus, they must learn to have inclusive love ("Love you must learn"), leading to the cessation of their isolation and identification with all humanity. They already have a dynamic

will and must learn to use that will in order to cooperate
("Dynamic will you have"). To have "the right use of destruction for the furtherance of the Plan," they must also learn to
follow the intuitive wisdom of the soul ("must be the way for
you"). By putting together these three characteristics of will,
love, and wisdom, they can render service that meets the needs
of humanity as a whole ("Adherence to the rhythm of the
planet"). This service will release them from the chaos of their
past and bring order into their experience ("will release the
hidden Blessed One and order bring").

In the last paragraph, the phrase "the right use of destruction for the furtherance of the Plan" requires some additional
explanation. It is important to realize that destruction of the
form is a necessary ingredient in all evolutionary growth. The
word *form* is a general term that can refer to religious dogma
and theology; to political or economic ideology; and to an
educational system such as a secular institution, church organization, Masonic fraternity, or esoteric group. After a particular
form is built, that form is utilized for as long as possible. Eventually there comes the time when the form no longer serves the
indwelling life, when the structure atrophies, crystallizes, and
becomes vulnerable. The task of the first-ray worker is to
advance the divine plan by destroying the outmoded forms, so
that new forms can take their place. According to the Bible,
"the kingdom of heaven suffereth violence, and the violent take
it by force" (Matt. 11:12). The first-ray person is one of those
"violent" ones, attaining higher consciousness ("the kingdom of
heaven") through the right use of destructive energies.

Ray Two

The Blessed One built him an ark. Stage by stage he
built it, and floated upon the bosom of the waters.
Deeply he hid himself, and his light was no more
seen, — only his floating ark.

His voice was heard: "I have built and strongly built, but am a prisoner within my building. My light is hidden. Only my word goes forth. Around me lie the waters. Can I return from whence I came? Is the word strong enough to open wide the door? What shall I do?"

The answer came: "Build now an ark translucent, which can reveal the light, O Builder of the ark. And by that light you shall reveal the lighted way. The power to build anew, the right use of the Word, and the using of the light, — these will release the Blessed One, deep hidden in the ark."[7]

The second ray is called the ray of love-wisdom. The basic quality for individuals on this ray is inclusive love, and the basic technique is attracting what one needs. They have a desire for knowledge and truth, are more magnetic than dynamic, and are builders rather than destroyers. They generally have tact, foresight, and the ability to convey understanding to others. They may be excellent ambassadors, psychotherapists, teachers, or college heads. As soldiers, they would plan wisely and never lead their troops into danger through rashness, but they may be deficient in rapidity of action and energy. Artists on this ray would seek to teach through their art. As writers, their literary work would generally be instructive.[8]

During the stage of selfish influence, second-ray individuals have the power to build for self-centered ends ("The Blessed One built him an ark"), and they subordinate all their available soul powers to those ends. Stage by stage they build their desired surroundings ("Stage by stage he built it"), and they satisfy their longing for material well-being ("and floated upon the bosom of the waters"). Owing to the second-ray quality of their souls, they have the capacity to be sensitive to the needs of others. But because they choose to cultivate a separative spirit and remain apart ("Deeply he hid himself"), the light of the soul, which is the basic love nature, is no longer revealed ("and his light was no more seen"). Only their selfish desires and material attainments are apparent ("only his floating ark").

The second paragraph describes the crisis of evocation for the second ray. Persons undergoing this experience realize that they have built a comforting and secure material environment ("I have built and strongly built"), but that they have become attached and engrossed with that environment ("but am a prisoner within my building"). By having used some soul powers, they sense the basic quality of the soul, which is inclusive love, and realize that this quality lies hidden ("My light is hidden"). Although they would like to express their love nature, they realize that they have direct control over only their thoughts and speech ("Only my word goes forth"), not over the strong selfish feelings in which they are engulfed ("Around me lie the waters"). They ponder over a number of questions: Can they return to their basic love nature? Is the mental principle, working through the energy of thought and the spoken word, strong enough to open wide the door to expressing love ("Is the word strong enough to open wide the door")? What should they do? Their characteristic method of approaching the spiritual path is by seeking answers to these questions through close and earnest study of various psychological and spiritual teachings.

The third paragraph describes the unfoldment during the stage of group awareness. Because of their longing for wisdom and truth, second-ray individuals receive intuitive answers from the soul. They learn how to bring the personality to a point where it is simply a transparency, permitting the full shining forth of the inner spiritual nature ("Build now an ark translucent, which can reveal the light"), which requires that they rebuild each aspect of the personality ("O Builder of the ark"). When this process is completed, their inner light will reveal to others the reality of the spiritual path ("And by that light you shall reveal the lighted way"). There are three principal steps. The first step is building new habit patterns by learning to express virtuous behavior ("The power to build anew"). This type of behavior is based on renouncing the belief of separateness and being sensitive to the needs of others. The second step is invoking the wisdom of the soul ("the right use of the Word") for purifying the emotional body, guiding the words spoken to others, and determining all activities. And the third step is gaining true illumination by merging in consciousness with the soul ("and the using of the light"). By practicing these steps, they will free themselves from being engrossed with the material world and be able to build outer forms that express the divine plan ("these will release the Blessed One, deep hidden in the ark").

Ray Three

The Blessed One gathered force. He hid himself behind a veil. He rolled himself within that veil, and deeply hid his face. Naught could be seen but that which veiled, and active motion. Within that veil was latent thought.

The thought reached forth: "Behind this veil of maya I stand, a Blessed One, but unrevealed. My energy is great, and through my mind I can display the glory of divinity. How can I, therefore, demonstrate this truth? What shall I do? I wander in illusion."

The word went forth: "All is illusion, O Dweller in the shadows. Come forth into the light of day. Display the hidden glory of the Blessed One, the glory of the One and Only. The glory and the truth will rapidly destroy that which has veiled the truth. The prisoner can go free. The rending of the blinding veil, the clear pronouncing of the truth, and practice right will render to the Blessed One that golden thread which will provide release from all the maze of earth existence." [9]

The third ray is called the ray of active intelligence. The basic quality of a person on this ray is intellect, and the basic technique is selectively manipulating the elements of the environment. Persons on this ray have a highly developed faculty of imagination and can grasp the essence of a truth by the power of this faculty. Due to their wide views and great caution, they often see every side of a question equally clearly, which sometimes paralyzes their actions. They may be good abstract thinkers, philosophers, and business people. As soldiers, they would work out tactical problems at their desks but would seldom be outstanding on the field. As artists, their subjects would be full of thought and interest, but their technique may not be polished. As writers, their literary style would often be vague and involved. [10]

During the stage of selfish influence, third-ray individuals intelligently gather and use the forces of the environment ("The Blessed One gathered force"). They manipulate those forces with the motive of hiding behind a veil of glory, beauty, and material attainments ("He hid himself behind a veil"). As a result, they are involved with intense material and mental activity ("He rolled himself within that veil"), and they submerge themselves within illusions, glamours, and maya ("and deeply hid his face"). Nothing can be seen except the veil of their self-deception ("Naught could be seen but that which veiled") and the energy of their activity as an end in itself ("and active motion"). Behind that veil lies the creative intelligence of the soul, latent and unexpressed ("Within that veil was latent thought").

In this commentary, the terms *illusion*, *glamour*, and *maya* are used to denote three different types of distortions. An illusion is a false idea or concept, a belief or opinion that is not in accord with reality. A glamour is an emotional reaction that distorts perception, such as pride, self-pity, or criticism. The

Sanskrit word *maya* means illusion, but this word is given a special meaning in the context being considered here. While glamour is illusion that has been intensified by desire, maya is glamour that has been intensified by vital energy. For instance, maya is present when a person has a compulsion — an irrational repetitive behavior that is difficult to resist.[11]

The crisis of evocation occurs in the following way. Rather than thinking only about manipulating the material world, third-ray persons begin to have deeper thoughts ("The thought reached forth"). They sense intuitively that an inner divine nature exists behind the relative uselessness of their outer activities, but that this nature has not yet been revealed ("Behind this veil of maya I stand, a Blessed One, but unrevealed"). They feel that this inner nature is highly creative ("My energy is great") and that it can illuminate the mind ("and through my mind I can display the glory of divinity"). They inquire about how this inner nature can be revealed through the mind ("How can I, therefore, demonstrate this truth?") and through work in the outer world ("What should I do?"). Their characteristic method of approaching the spiritual path is through deep thinking along these philosophic lines until certain realizations are achieved. Because they are aware of wandering in illusions and glamours ("I wander in illusion"), they call on their inner nature for guidance during this inquiry.

The third paragraph refers to the stage of group awareness. Owing to their desire for right revelation of divinity and light, third-ray individuals receive intuitive thoughts from the soul. They learn that their perceptions have been distorted by glamours and illusions ("All is illusion"), because they have been focused in the personality ("O Dweller in the shadows"). They also learn how to eliminate these distortions. The first step is observing the personality from the vantage point of the soul ("Come forth in the light of day"), which means observing without judgment, criticism, or resistance. The second step is using the basic technique of the soul, which is selective manipulation ("Display the hidden glory of the Blessed One"), to disengage from all physical activities except those that cooperate with humanity as a whole ("the glory of the One and Only"). The third step is using the illumined mind to destroy glamours, and the fourth step is using the wisdom of the soul to destroy illusions ("The glory and the truth will rapidly destroy that which has veiled the truth"). By practicing these steps, they can free themselves from their physical, emotional, and mental entanglements ("The prisoner can go free").

After achieving a certain measure of freedom from their own distortions, they can begin working to further the divine plan. The first step is intuitively receiving ideas that will unlock some door in science, psychology, or religion ("The rending of the blinding veil"). This door, when opened, will bring release or relief to many. The second step is clearly expressing the new ideas in speech and writing—avoiding ambiguity, half thoughts, innuendos, and suggestions ("the clear pronouncing of the truth"). Because third-ray people have developed the habit of guarding themselves with devious formulations of thoughts and ideas, they have difficulty in conveying their meaning clearly and must make an effort to do so.[12] And the third step is the practical application and demonstration of the new ideas ("practice right"), which involves selectively gathering needed materials and then adapting those materials for the helping of the world.

The expression "that golden thread" in the last sentence of the statement requires some additional explanation. A fundamental teaching of theosophy is that the solar system can be divided into seven worlds, called *planes*, and each of these can be divided into seven *subplanes*. For instance, the physical is the lowest plane, and it can be divided into the following subplanes: first ether, second ether, third ether, fourth ether, gaseous, liquid, and solid. The three lowest subplanes—gaseous, liquid, and solid—compose the dense world of matter and are perceptible with the five physical senses. The four highest subplanes represent the etheric region. Although imperceptible with normal faculties, these four ethers are considered part of the physical realm.

Corresponding to the division of the physical plane into dense and etheric portions, a person's physical body also has two portions. The *dense physical body* is composed of solids, liquids, and gases, including such parts as the bones, blood system, nervous system, brain, and endocrine glands. The *etheric body* is composed of the four ethers and is sometimes called the vital body. It is referred to in the Bible as the "golden bowl" (Eccles. 12:6). According to Bailey, the etheric body is composed of golden lines of energy and of centers that are formed by the crossing of these lines.[13] In Sanskrit, the lines of energy are called *nadis*, and the centers of energy are called *chakras*.

Consequently, the expression "that golden thread" in the last sentence of the statement can be interpreted as referring to the etheric body. The chakras in the etheric body evolve over time and move from a sluggish semidormant state to an active fully developed state. When the earlier sets of steps are practiced, the etheric chakras naturally and automatically become developed. As a result, the person will be able to direct and manipulate the forces in the etheric body, which in turn will provide release from maya or illusion on etheric levels ("will render to the Blessed One that golden thread which will provide release from all the maze of earth existence"). Through this process, the person will be able to work effectively and efficiently in the outer world, employing only those forces and energies that serve the intended purpose.

Ray Four

The Blessed One rushed forth to combat. He saw existence as two warring forces, and fought them both. Loaded with the panoply of war, he stood midway, looking two ways. The clash of battle, the many weapons he had learned to use, the longing not to fight, the thrill of finding those he fought were but brothers and himself, the anguish of defeat, the paean of his victory, — these held him down.

The Blessed One paused and questioned: "Whence come the victory and whence defeat? Am I not the Blessed One Himself? I will invoke the angels to my aid."

The trumpet sound went forth: "Rise up and fight, and reconcile the armies of the Lord. There is no battle. Force the conflict to subside; send for the invocation for the peace of all; form out of two, one army of the Lord; let victory crown the efforts of the Blessed One by harmonising all. Peace lies behind the warring energies."[14]

The fourth ray is called the ray of harmony through conflict. The basic quality of a fourth-ray individual is harmony and synthesis, and the basic technique is unifying the forces in the environment. This ray is also called the "ray of struggle" because individuals on this ray often have personalities that are torn between conflicting tendencies, such as the love of ease, pleasure, indolence, and procrastination on the one hand and fiery impatience and urge to action on the other. They may be wild speculators and gamblers who are full of enthusiasm and plans, become easily overwhelmed by failure, but quickly recover from their misfortunes. As soldiers, they would tend to disregard risks to themselves and their followers; as artists, their sense of color would be great, but their drawing might be defective; as musicians, their music would be full of melody; and as writers, their literary work would often be brilliant and full of picturesque word-paintings but might be inaccurate and full of exaggerations.[15]

The first paragraph of Bailey's statement describes the stage of selfish influence. By applying the intuitive perception of the soul to what occurs outside themselves, fourth-ray persons sense that human beings have a noble function, namely, establishing harmony, peace, and beauty within humanity as a whole and within all of nature. Owing to this sensitivity, they rush forth into confused combat with a constant series of dilemmas ("The Blessed One rushed forth to combat"). They think of each dilemma as a choice between a higher way and a lower way regarding some issue ("He saw existence as two warring forces"), while feeling that neither alternative is satisfactory ("and fought them both"). The higher way is based upon a sensed responsibility to humanity, and the lower way is based upon their own self-interest. They do not wish to choose the higher way because they are not yet ready to make the self-sacrifice and self-denial that they feel would be required. But they do not wish to choose the lower way because that would not be in harmony with their new sense of responsibility.

For instance, they may think of one dilemma as a choice between selflessness, such as donating wealth to the poor, and selfishness, such as enjoying possessions. Or perhaps it is between suppressing and indulging negative feelings, or between appeasing and opposing some tyrant, or between love and hate. Many other examples could be given. Each dilemma is characterized as being a choice between what is called a "pair of opposites." The only way that any such pair of opposites can be satisfactorily resolved is by finding a middle path that lies between the two opposites: for instance, a middle choice that is neither selflessness nor selfishness, neither suppression nor indulgence, neither appeasing nor opposing, and neither love nor hate. But to find this middle path, it is necessary to evoke the wisdom of the soul.[16]

However, during the stage of selfish influence, fourth-ray persons do not try to find the middle path between the opposites. Instead, as described by the rest of the first paragraph, they struggle with these dilemmas while being "loaded with the panoply of war." The word *panoply* means a suit of armor, and it refers to the various defense mechanisms that they employ, such as intellectual analysis, rationalization, and suppression. The darkness of confusion veils their intuition, and they cooperate with the alternative that can be more readily justified ("he stood midway, looking two ways"). Because they have decided to cooperate with the part and not the whole, they sense inharmony within themselves. Owing to this inner struggle ("The clash of battle") and their many defense mechanisms ("the many weapons he had learned to use"), they long for not having to choose one alternative over another ("the longing not to fight"). Because they feel identified with all humanity ("the thrill of finding those he fought were but brothers and himself"), they experience anguish when there is suffering among any group of people ("the anguish of defeat"). Just as they use defense mechanisms to avoid facing conflicts inside themselves, they also give undue recognition to words of harmony between themselves and others ("the paean of his victory"), rather than to any underlying divisive issues. All of these factors cause them to feel confused and depressed ("these held him down").

By applying the intuitive perception of the soul to their own inner struggle, fourth-ray persons undergo the crisis of evocation. As described by the second paragraph, they pause in this struggle and ask: Why must there be outcomes in which one aspect of the self is victorious and another one defeated ("Whence come the victory and whence defeat")? Sensing that their inner nature is harmony and synthesis ("Am I not the Blessed One Himself?"), they decide to invoke that nature to achieve outcomes in which the warring forces within are unified ("I will invoke the angels to my aid"). Their characteristic manner of approaching the spiritual path is through practicing self-control with the goal of gaining inner equilibrium.

For instance, they may become involved with hatha yoga, which is a discipline aimed at achieving mastery over the physical body. Because the physical and mental bodies are closely interrelated, the control of nervous and vital energies can lead to the control of mental functions. The Sanskrit word *hatha* is derived from the roots *ha*, meaning "sun," and *tha*, meaning "moon." Thus, hatha can be translated as the equalization and stabilization of the "sun breath," referring to the breath flowing through the right nostril, and the "moon breath," referring to the breath flowing through the left nostril. The principal steps of hatha yoga are *asana* and *pranayama*. Asana consists of maintaining certain physical postures, such as the lotus position, head stand, shoulder stand, and so forth. Pranayama refers to the control and regulation of the vital energy through various breathing exercises.[17]

According to the third paragraph, the inner wisdom of the soul is evoked during the stage of group awareness ("The trumpet sound went forth"). Fourth-ray individuals learn that they must first "rise up" above their emotional glamours, which means to ponder them with the mental body while being guided by the soul, and then use the resulting illumination to dissipate those glamours ("and fight"). Through this process, they can reconcile the warring forces within themselves ("reconcile the armies of the Lord") and discover "there is no battle" among the essential interests that underlie those forces.

After first resolving their inner conflicts, they can turn their attention to resolving disputes occurring between warring groups of people. The remaining portion of the third paragraph lists the following steps: force any actual fighting to subside ("Force the conflict to subside"); organize a conference which seeks a just peace for all parties ("send for the invocation for the peace of all"); by helping the opposing sides to communicate and develop an attitude of mutual respect, form a single working group at the conference ("form out of two, one army of the Lord"); and by using right judgment and pure reason, formulate an agreement that integrates the essential interests of all parties ("let victory crown the efforts of the Blessed One by harmonising all"). The key to implementing the last step is realizing that the essential interests of the warring parties are not conflicting, because their souls are not conflicting ("Peace lies behind the warring energies").

Ray Five

The Blessed One came forth in ignorance. He wandered in a darkness deep of spirit. He saw no reason for this way of life. He sought among the many threads that weave the outer garment of the Lord, and found the many ways there be, leading to the centre of the web eternal. The forms that weave that web hide the divine reality. He lost himself. Fear entered in.

He asked himself: "Another pattern must be woven; another garment formed. What shall I do? Shew me another way to weave."

The Word for him came forth in triple form. His mind responded to the vision clear evoked: — "The truth lies hidden in the unknown Way. The Angel of the Presence guards that Way. The mind reveals the Angel and the door. Stand in that Presence. Lift up thine eyes. Enter through that golden door. Thus will the Angel, who is the shadow of the Blessed One, reveal the open door. That Angel too must disappear. The Blessed One remains and passes through that door into the light sublime."[18]

The fifth ray is called the ray of concrete knowledge or science. The basic quality for individuals on this ray is discrimination, and their technique is differentiating the elements in their environment. As a result, they have keen intellects, are accurate in details, and make unwearied efforts to verify every theory. Other characteristics include being orderly, punctual, businesslike, and sometimes pedantic. They may be excellent scientists who analyze the material world in terms of causes and effects, or excellent electricians, engineers, or operating surgeons. As soldiers, they would be interested in artillery and engineering. As artists, which is rare, their coloring would be dull, sculptures lifeless, and music uninteresting though technically correct in form. As writers, their style would be extreme clarity, but lacking fire and often being long-winded.[19]

When entering the stage of selfish influence, fifth-ray individuals are ignorant concerning the essential spiritual nature of themselves and of other human beings ("The Blessed One came forth in ignorance"). Due to their innate quality of discrimination, they are critical of themselves and others, rationalize their failings, and mentally separate themselves from others ("He wandered in a darkness deep of spirit"). Because they do not understand the meaning or purpose of life ("He saw no reason for this way of life"), they seek answers by making a detailed analysis of the material world ("He sought among the many threads that weave the outer garment of the Lord"). They find many lines of inquiry to follow, and each of these could lead to the inference that a nonmaterial life is at the center of the material world ("and found the many ways there be, leading to the centre of the web eternal"). However, their acquired knowledge produces an intense materialism that hides the underlying spiritual reality ("The forms that weave that web hide the divine reality") and further isolates them from others ("He lost himself"). Owing to the anxiety that results from this wrong emphasis ("Fear entered in"), they have distorted perceptions of the world.

The second paragraph describes the crisis of evocation. Through their material investigations, fifth-ray individuals awaken their inner understanding and infer the existence of a nonmaterial life. They differentiate between the material world about which they have direct knowledge and the nonmaterial life about which they can only infer. They realize that another pattern of knowledge must be constructed ("Another pattern must be woven") and new theories formed regarding that nonmaterial life ("another garment formed"). Being uncertain about what should be done ("What shall I do?"), they call on their inner understanding to show how this new kind of knowledge can be acquired ("Shew me another way to weave"). Their characteristic manner of approaching the spiritual path is through scientific research, pushed to ultimate conclusions, and accepting the inferences that follow.

To understand the symbolism in Bailey's next paragraph, it is necessary to give some additional definitions. According to theosophy, the mental plane consists of seven subplanes which are divided into two groups: the lowest four subplanes are the concrete levels, and the top three subplanes are the abstract levels. An individual is said to have three focal points of perception on these subplanes. One focal point of perception is *the mental body*, sometimes called the lower concrete mind or simply the mind; it consists of matter from the lowest four subplanes. The mental body is concerned with concrete thoughts and facts. Another focal point of perception is *the soul*, sometimes called the causal body or egoic lotus; it consists of matter from the second and third divisions (counting from the top) of the mental plane. The soul is the storehouse for wisdom, which is the abstracted essence gained from a person's experience, and it is the instrument for expressing principles or abstract thoughts. The third focal point of perception is *the spiritual mind*, sometimes called the higher abstract mind; it consists of matter from only the highest mental subplane. The spiritual mind can convey insights, or direct perceptions of truth, that reflect the innate divine nature with clarity, synthesis, and inclusiveness. After receiving insights from the spiritual mind, the soul can then use those insights to guide its own expression of abstract thinking, which in turn can guide the concrete thinking of the mental body.[20]

The third paragraph describes the stage of group awareness. Intuitions come forth as a threefold synthesis of concrete thoughts from the mental body, wisdom or abstract thoughts from the soul, and insights from the spiritual mind ("The Word for him came forth in triple form"). Through evoking clear intuitions, fifth-ray individuals learn the following lessons ("His mind responded to the vision clear evoked"). They must develop the ability to receive insights, because knowledge of divinity lies hidden in a dimension that exists beyond the memories of both concrete facts and abstract principles ("The truth lies hidden in the unknown Way"). To develop this ability, they must have a realization of the soul and its potentialities ("The Angel of the Presence guards that Way"), which in turn requires that power be developed in the mental body to recognize and contact the soul ("The mind reveals the Angel and the door"). Thus, they must achieve two different alignments: between the soul and the spiritual mind ("Stand in that Presence"), and between the mental body and the soul ("Lift up thine eyes").

The remainder of the third paragraph describes how these alignments can be achieved. The first step is shifting the polarization of consciousness temporarily into the soul ("Enter through that golden door"). The second step is allowing the soul ("Thus will the Angel"), which is an outer aspect of the individual ("who is the shadow of the Blessed One"), to reveal the deeper reality of the spiritual mind ("reveal the open door"). And the third step is negating the activity of the soul ("That Angel too must disappear"). Through practicing these steps, fifth-ray individuals develop the power to shift the polarization of consciousness temporarily into the spiritual mind ("The Blessed One remains and passes through that door"), enabling them to attain direct knowledge of divinity ("into the light sublime").

Ray Six

The Blessed One caught the vision of the Way, and followed the Way without discretion. Fury characterised his efforts. The way led down into the world of dual life. Between the pairs of opposites, he took his stand, and as he swung pendent between them, fleeting glimpses of the goal shone forth. He swung in mid-heaven. He sought to swing into that radiant place of light, where stood the door upon the higher *Way*. But ever he swung between the pairs of opposites.

He spoke at last within himself: "I cannot seem to find the Way. I try this way, and tread with force that way, and always with the keenest wish. I try all ways. What shall I do to find *The Way*?"

A cry went forth. It seemed to come from deep within his heart: "Tread thou, O Pilgrim on the Way of sensuous life, the middle, lighted way. It passes straight between the dual worlds. Find thou that narrow, middle way. It leads you to your goal. Seek that perceptive steadiness which leads to proved endurance. Adherence to the chosen Way, and ignoring of the pairs of opposites, will bring this Blessed One upon the lighted way into the joy of proved success."[21]

The sixth ray is called the ray of devotion or idealism. The basic quality of individuals on this ray is sensitivity to the spiritual reality lying behind the phenomenal world. Their basic technique is devotional response, referring to a one-pointed application of desire and intelligence to produce an expression of the sensed idea. Consequently, the sixth is the ray of the devotee and idealist. Individuals on this ray have intense personal feelings and religious instincts. They are seldom great statesmen or business people, but may be great preachers or orators. As soldiers, they would hate fighting, but when aroused would fight with ferocity. As artists, they would be devoted to beauty and color, but their productive skill may not be very good. As writers, they would be poets of the emotions, perhaps with a religious theme.[22]

Individuals on both the fourth and sixth rays are involved with "the pair of opposites," but with different kinds. As discussed previously, the fourth-ray individual struggles with the pair of opposites in the form of a dilemma: choosing between higher and lower ways regarding some issue. As discussed next, the sixth-ray individual is involved with the pair of opposites in the form of partisanship.

The first paragraph of the statement corresponds to the stage of selfish influence. Sixth-ray individuals use the basic quality of the soul to appreciate some idea, or higher intuitive value, and then to formulate that idea into an ideal or vision ("The Blessed One caught the vision of the Way"). They next use their basic technique by becoming devoted to that ideal or vision. For instance, they may become devoted followers of Christ, Buddha, or someone else. Or they may become identified with some political, economic, or social ideal that purportedly can improve the human condition. However, they adhere to that vision with shortsighted blindness ("and followed the Way without discretion"), resulting in fanaticism, violence, militarism, and a tendency to make trouble with others and with groups ("Fury characterised his efforts"). Their shortsightedness leads down to partisanship ("The way led down into the world of dual life"). They consider people as friends or enemies, depending on the sympathy or lack of sympathy shown to their vision. Unable to see any viewpoint except their own, they are suspicious of other people's motives. They are willing to lay down their lives for the objects of their devotion or reverence but are unwilling to make any effort to help those outside their immediate sympathies.

The rest of the first paragraph emphasizes that a valid intuitive idea lies behind this misdirected devotion. By abstracting their consciousness from the material or form side of life ("Between the pair of opposites"), sixth-ray individuals achieved some alignment with the soul ("he took his stand"). As they focused their attention on the formless expression of truth ("as he swung pendent between them"), they intuitively sensed glimpses of some noble idea and goal ("fleeting glimpses of the goal shone forth"). But by losing the original intuitive idea in the formulated ideal and then becoming preoccupied with the method of implementing that ideal, they rapidly reacted to glamour and illusion ("He swung in mid-heaven"). They sought to express some noble idea and goal ("He sought to swing into that radiant place of light"), which would open the door to a higher way of life ("where stood the door upon the higher Way"). But they express only bewildered idealism, emotional devotion, and the partisan spirit ("But ever he swung between the pairs of opposites").

The crisis of evocation for the sixth ray occurs in the following way. These individuals eventually acknowledge that they cannot find a way to produce an expression of their particular ideals ("I cannot seem to find the Way"). They have tried promoting their own ideals ("I try this way") and tried attacking with fervor opposing ideals ("and tread with force that way"), always with dedicated commitment ("and always with the keenest wish"). They have now tried all the ways that seem to be possible, while producing only conflict and futility ("I try all ways"). Consequently, they ask within themselves what they should do to find a more effective way ("What shall I do to find The Way"). Their characteristic manner of approaching the spiritual path is through prayer and meditation, enabling them to become receptive to the guidance of the soul.

As was discussed during the commentary for the third ray, the physical body can be divided into etheric and dense portions. The word *chakra* means "wheel" in Sanskrit, and it generally refers to a subtle wheel of energy, or force center, in the etheric body that vitalizes a portion of the dense physical body. Because Bailey's symbolic passages occasionally refer to the chakras, it may be helpful to review some information about them. There are said to be seven major etheric chakras. According to Bailey, these chakras are part of that portion of the etheric body that lies outside the dense physical body. In particular, the crown chakra is "just above the top of the head." The brow chakra is "just in front of the eyes and forehead." The five spinal chakras are the throat, heart, solar plexus, sacral, and basic, and these are positioned in the "etheric counterpart of the spinal column," which is behind the dense physical spine. The spinal centers are at least two inches away from the dense physical spine for an undeveloped person and are even farther away for an average person.[23]

The third paragraph describes the stage of group awareness. The light of the soul breaks in and provides intuitive instruction ("A cry went forth"). This light includes the qualities associated with the heart chakra, namely love, inclusiveness, plus understanding ("It seems to come from deep within his heart"). In the past, sixth-ray individuals made decisions based on the reactions of the personality ("O Pilgrim on the Way of sensuous life"). Now they learn that they must follow the lighted way, which means having the mind illumined by the light of the soul ("Tread thou the middle, lighted way"). This way is the middle way because it is concerned with inclusion and not separation, with peace and not war, and with the good of the whole and not the part ("It passes straight between the dual worlds"). This way is also narrow because it passes between partisan groups without taking sides ("Find thou that narrow, middle way"). For instance, when standing between the exploited and the exploiting, the warlike and the pacifist, or the masses and the rulers, there must be no partisan spirit, no fomenting of political or religious disturbances, and no feeding of hatred for individuals, nations, or races. This approach leads to a demonstration of right human relations, the basic oneness of humanity, practical brotherhood, and positive harmlessness ("It leads you to your goal").

The remainder of the third paragraph describes the steps needed for following the lighted way. The first step is deliberately acquiring such virtues as tolerance, balance, serenity, and common sense ("Seek that perceptual steadiness"), which enables a true spiritual unfoldment to occur ("which leads to proved endurance"). The second step is holding firmly to the guidance of the soul, while developing breadth of vision and eliminating any glamours ("Adherence to the chosen Way"). And the third step is ignoring all outer barriers and separative differences in mental ideas and material ways of living ("and ignoring of the pairs of opposites"). By following these steps,

sixth-ray individuals will gain sympathy with the viewpoints of
other people, be willing to see the work of others progress along
their chosen lines, and be effective in expressing their own
ideals ("will bring this Blessed One upon the lighted way into
the joy of proved success").

Ray Seven

The Blessed One sought the pathway into form, but
held with firmness to the hand of the Magician. He
sought to reconcile the Pilgrim, who was himself, to
life in form. He sought to bring the world of disorder
in which he found himself into some kind of order.
He wandered far into the deepest depths and became
immersed in chaos and disorder. He could not understand, yet still held to the hand of the Magician. He
sought to bring about that order that his soul craved.
He talked with all he met, but his bewilderment
increased.

To the Magician thus he spoke: "The ways of the
Creator must be good. Behind all that which seems to
be, must be a Plan. Teach me the purpose of it all.
How can I work, immersed in deepest matter? Tell
me the thing that I must do?"

The Magician said: "Listen, O Worker in the furthest world, to the rhythm of the times. Note the
pulsation in the heart of that which is divine. Retire
into the silence and attune yourself unto the whole.
Then venture forth. Establish the right rhythm; bring
order to the forms of life which must express the Plan
of Deity."

For this Blessed One release is found in work. He
must display his knowledge of the Plan by the sounding of those words which will evoke the Builders of
the forms and thus create the new.[24]

The seventh ray is called the ray of ceremonial order or magic. The basic quality for individuals on the seventh ray is magic, which in this context means the ability to unify a mental image with the tangible form or appearance. Their basic technique is coordinating, blending, and fusing the elements of the physical world. As a result, they take delight in doing things decently and in order, according to rule and precedent. For instance, nurses for the sick would be using magical abilities, in the sense intended here, when they carefully implement in the smallest detail their mental picture of how an ideal hospital environment would look. With their organizing power, seventh-ray individuals might be excellent business people. As soldiers, they would dress and feed the troops in the best possible way. As artists or sculptors, they would produce ideal beauty in material forms and patterns. As writers, their style would be ultrapolished, but they might be concerned more about style than content.[25]

The first paragraph corresponds to the stage of selfish influence. Because of their efforts to achieve material success ("The Blessed One sought the pathway into form"), seventh-ray individuals have unfolded sufficient powers of the soul to perform magic ("but held with firmness to the hand of the Magician"). In other words, in the context of their chosen profession, they are able to manifest material forms which reflect their mental images. However, they are involved with *black magic*, which is the use of magical powers to satisfy the self-centered ends of the personality ("He sought to reconcile the Pilgrim, who was himself, to life in form"). By using their magical powers, they try to bring the disorder in their personal lives into some kind of order ("He sought to bring the world of disorder in which he found himself into some kind of order"). But due to their egotistical motivations ("He wandered far into the deepest depths"), they produce more confusion and disorder for themselves ("and became immersed in chaos and disorder"). They do not use the intuitive understanding of the soul to select their mental images ("He could not understand"), and yet they use the powers of the soul to manifest those images ("yet still held to the hand of the Magician"). Thus, they are involved with untruth, perversion of soul powers, and possibly sex magic, where the latter refers to transforming mental sexual fantasies into material fulfillment. Even though they do not understand the plan of the soul, they seek to bring about the order that would satisfy the basic nature of the soul ("He sought to bring about that order that his soul craved").

The last sentence of the first paragraph indicates that the use of speech creates some additional problems. As described further in chapter 2, there is a close connection between speech and magical work. Through speech, a thought is evoked and becomes present; this thought is brought out of a nebulous condition and then becomes materialized into something very definite, called a *thoughtform*, on the etheric levels of the physical plane. During the stage of selfish influence, seventh-ray persons are faced with the difficulty of being able to enforce their words with strength, creating thoughtforms that are strongly vitalized and exceedingly clear-cut. However, they generally do not understand the significance of speech, when to speak, and what happens when they speak. Because their speech is frequently purposeless or motivated by self-centered considerations ("He talked with all he met"), the created thoughtforms are often not worthwhile. This wrong use of speech is apt to disrupt any group work, be a destructive force in the world, and increase confusion ("but his bewilderment increased").[26]

The crisis of evocation occurs in the following way. Due to the basic quality of the soul, which is magic, seventh-ray individuals intuitively sense that order must exist in the universe ("The ways of the Creator must be good"), implying that a divine plan must exist behind the material world ("Behind all that which seems to be, must be a Plan"). Because their own activities have produced additional confusion and disorder, they call on their inner understanding to reveal the purpose of that plan ("Teach me the purpose of it all"), how they on the physical plane can help in manifesting it ("How can I work,

immersed in deepest matter?"), and what they must do to prepare themselves for this work ("Tell me the thing that I must
do?"). Their characteristic manner of approaching the spiritual
path is to bring order into their own lives through the observance of certain rules of practice and ritual. For example, they
may use particular forms of meditation at particular times of
the day, including affirmations that affect the subconscious
mind.

During the stage of group awareness, the soul provides
intuitive instruction ("The Magician said") on how to become
an effective worker in the physical world ("O Worker in the
furthest world"). The first step is listening to the motives of the
personality and discovering the times when there is material
mindedness, selfish ambition, or unloving behavior ("Listen to
the rhythm of the times"). The second step is becoming attuned
to the activity of the heart chakra ("Note the pulsation in the
heart of that which is divine"). This step requires subordinating
such vices as formalism, narrowness, and pride, and instead
becoming identified with the spiritual reality lying behind the
material world. The third step is deepening the practice of
meditation ("Retire into the silence") and developing the power
to cooperate with the divine plan ("and attune yourself unto the
whole"). The divine plan is received in the form of an intuitive
understanding of the world need and how to meet that need.
However, the mind must be used to convert the intuitive ideas
into concrete pictures, something that can be visualized. The
fourth step is practicing *white magic*, or the use of soul powers
for spiritual ends, by manifesting those mental pictures in the
physical world ("Then venture forth"). By accomplishing these
steps, seventh-ray individuals establish right order through
right magic ("Establish the right rhythm") and build material
forms that express the divine plan ("bring order to the forms of
life which must express the Plan of Deity").

The seventh ray statement is the only one that includes a
fourth paragraph. According to the first portion of this paragraph, seventh-ray persons find their release by relating the

spiritual and material dimensions of life ("For this Blessed One release is found in work"). They must display their knowledge of the divine plan by building the material forms needed for implementing the purposes of the other rays ("He must display his knowledge of the Plan"). For instance, in the field of government, they work in collaboration with the first-ray workers. In the field of religion, they build those forms that enable the second- and sixth-ray activities to be expressed. In the field of business, they cooperate with the third-ray workers. In the field of conflict resolution, they help to manifest the fourth-ray activities. And in the field of science, they assist the fifth-ray workers.

The second portion of the fourth paragraph describes a basic and fundamental principle by which all white magic is governed: by applying the proper and correct stimulation to the center called the soul of any form ("by the sounding of those words which will evoke the Builders of the forms"), but not to the form itself, that stimulated center will do its own work of destruction, attraction, and rebuilding ("and thus create the new"). In other words, white magic is concerned with the unfoldment of the soul within the form, rather than with direct work on the form. This principle is applicable to the soul of a human being, the soul of a nation, the soul of humanity itself, and the soul functioning in any form in every kingdom of nature. The point is that seventh-ray workers must utilize this principle when they help manifest the divine plan.[27]

The discussion for each ray given in this chapter has been quite brief. The next chapter expands and elaborates on these ideas.

Chapter 2

Techniques of Integration

Following birth, a human being learns to integrate the etheric body with the dense physical body, the emotional body with the etheric body, and then the mental body with the emotional body. After learning how to coordinate all aspects of the personality, we begin the process of integrating personality with soul. This last stage of integration takes the individual through certain expansions of awareness that in theosophy are called initiations. It is possible to relate each initiation to a specific stage of development in Christian mysticism, Hinduism, or Buddhism. It is also possible to relate each initiation to increased activity in a specific chakra, as explained next.

Bailey states that each major etheric chakra is separated from the one above it and the one below it by an interlaced protected web of etheric substance. When intact, these webs prevent the free movement of energies in the etheric body. As we purify our lives, discipline our emotions, and practice meditation, these webs become dissipated normally and automatically. Each web can be thought of as representing a specific lesson, learning, or realization. When this lesson is mastered, the uprising of energies in the etheric body dissipates the web and reaches the next higher chakra. As a result, that chakra is considered as being developed, and we attain a higher state of consciousness.[1]

For instance, when the web between the solar plexus chakra and heart chakra is dissipated, the heart chakra is said to be developed, and we attain the first spiritual initiation, sometimes called "Birth at Bethlehem." When the web between the heart chakra and throat chakra is dissipated, the throat chakra is developed, and we attain the second initiation, called "Baptism in Jordan." And when the web between the throat chakra and brow chakra is dissipated, the brow chakra is developed, and we attain the third initiation, called "Transfiguration." This last initiation is sometimes referred to as the opening of the third eye.[2]

The process of integrating personality with soul is intuitively guided by the soul. Because there are seven basic types of souls, there are seven basic processes of integration—one for each ray. Each process extends from the stage of selfish influence through the third initiation. The requirements for each initiation are discussed in this chapter, and it is shown how these requirements differ from ray to ray. The term *aspirant* denotes someone on the path of probation prior to the first initiation; *disciple*, someone on the path of discipleship between the first and third initiations; and *initiate*, someone who has attained the third initiation.

It is convenient to divide the process of integration for each ray into seven distinct stages:

1. *Selfish influence.* By using some of their soul powers, individuals during this stage coordinate their personalities and achieve their selfish ambitions. But because they have not sought to be guided by the wisdom of the soul, the ray force of the soul is expressed in a wrong and distorted manner.

2. *Crisis of evocation.* Because some alignment has been achieved, aspirants can sense intuitively the basic quality of the soul's ray. The inconsistency between their daily life and their

sensed potential brings them to a point of inner crisis where they begin to evoke the guidance of the soul. This point marks the beginning of what is called the path of probation.

3. *Self-observation.* Aspirants begin to see the need for observing their personalities in a detached and objective manner. At first they spasmodically take stock of their situation, but later they are able to make an honest assessment of their activities and discover their underlying motives.

4. *Reorientation.* Through a combination of self-observation and careful reasoning, aspirants discover the weaknesses, or vices, that they express and the opposite qualities, or virtues, that they need to acquire. Each vice is a distorted expression of the same ray force that can appear also as a virtue. By reorienting and rebuilding their mental, emotional, and physical natures, they transmute the vices into virtues. This transmutation requires calling in new motives and a new vibratory rhythm, so the soul can become the controlling factor.

5. *First initiation.* When the first initiation is attained, the path of probation is completed and the path of discipleship begins. Because their alignment has increased, disciples are guided more consistently by the soul. In particular, they are guided to work consciously at dissipating their glamours, where the word *glamour* refers to an emotional reaction that prevents clear perception. In the previous stage the emphasis was on learning to express new virtues, but now the emphasis is on using the illumined mind to discover, understand, and dissipate the emotional reactions that underlie the vices. Although the method of dissipating glamours is similar for each ray, the glamours that must be dissipated vary from ray to ray.

6. *Second initiation.* After they attain the second initiation, disciples become ready to deepen their practice of meditation. Their first step is to draw consciousness away from both the physical and emotional bodies into the realm of concrete thought, or the mental body. After achieving that step, their

effort is to transcend the lower mind and become temporarily polarized in the realm of abstract thought, or the soul. After achieving that step, they then follow the particular form of meditation appropriate for the soul's ray.

7. *Third initiation*. When the third initiation is attained, the path of discipleship is completed. Initiates have integrated personality and soul, which means that their normal polarization is in the soul. Having attained group consciousness, they are ready to begin a new cycle of work, leading to still higher expansions of consciousness in the future.

Alice A. Bailey has published, without interpretation, a symbolic statement for each ray, which she called the "Technique of Integration." Each of these statements can be thought of as being a continuation of the corresponding one given in the previous chapter. Under the heading for each ray in chapter 1, the following stages were described: the stage of selfish influence, the crisis of evocation, and the stage of group awareness. Under the heading for each ray in this chapter, Bailey's Technique of Integration is given first and then followed by an interpretation that elaborates in detail the various subdivisions occurring within the stage of group awareness.

Ray One

The love of power must dominate. There must also be repudiation of those forms which wield no power.

The word goes forth from soul to form; "Stand up. Press outward into life. Achieve a goal. For you, there must be not a circle, but a line.

"Prepare *the form*. Let the eyes look forward, not on either side. Let the ears be closed to all the outer voices, and the hands clenched, the body braced, and mind alert. Emotion is not used in furthering of the Plan. Love takes its place."

The symbol of a moving point of light appears above the brow. The keynote of the life though uttered not, yet still is clearly heard: "I move to power. I am the One. We are a Unity in power. And all is for the power and glory of the *One*." [3]

The first ray is that of will, or power, and it is the ray of born leaders. During the stage of selfish influence, first-ray persons are one-pointed, unalterable, and undeviating. They move relentlessly forward to achieve their ambitions, destroying and tearing down what others have built so that they might rise to greater heights. However, this ruthlessness leads to feelings of being isolated and separated from other people.

Because they have been using some of their soul powers, first-ray persons eventually know in their brain consciousness that they have contacted the soul: they become aware of being a living principle of divinity with a responsibility to the whole of humanity. Due to this awareness, they experience the crisis of evocation and begin to search within themselves for answers.

The first step for aspirants on the path of probation is observing their activities from the vantage point of the soul. It is as though a curtain were raised, enabling the light of objective observation to break in. They see that they have trampled on other people and their destinies. They also see that their activities have not made any real contribution to humanity but have served only to gratify their own separative ambitions.

The next step for aspirants is to begin a careful process of reasoning in which they *discover for themselves* the roots of their problem. Although they may receive advice, hints, and suggestions from various books and teachers, they must reason the matter out for themselves by evoking the wisdom of the soul. Bailey's Technique of Integration begins with this step. As outlined in the first paragraph, first-ray aspirants come to the following conclusion: to serve others in an effective way, "the love of power must dominate." Because the purity of the intent determines the potency, this phrase means that it is important to examine one's motives and establish the single purpose of rendering true service. A mixed motive limits the effectiveness of any effort. A single or pure motive is rare, and where it exists there is always success and achievement. Another conclusion is that there must be the elimination of all impediments to maintaining singleness of purpose ("There must also be repudiation of those forms which wield no power"). These impediments include such vices as pride, ambition, arrogance, willfulness, and the desire to control others. Rather than struggling with these vices, it is more effective to apply with determination and persistence the opposite qualities, or virtues: humility, sympathy, tolerance, patience, and tenderness. Chapter 3 describes several meditation exercises that can be used to help apply these virtues.[4]

The first-ray technique places very little emphasis on the probationary path. By comparing the symbolic statements for the various rays, it can be seen that the first-ray technique has the fewest number of words dedicated to that particular stage. The reason is that first-ray aspirants can use their powerful will to make the necessary changes with relative ease once they understand that their vices are personality limitations.

When there has been success in this process of reorientation, the disciple completes the path of probation, attains the first initiation, and begins the path of discipleship. As described in the second paragraph of the technique, intuitive instruction goes forth from soul to personality ("The word goes forth from soul to form"). The disciple learns to "stand up," or increase alignment with the soul, so that clarity of thought can be achieved regarding difficult problems; "press outward into life," or become more inclusive, by contacting and understanding other people; and "achieve a goal" of being able to render service with complete impersonality, which would fulfill the earlier purpose. The lesson is also given that "there must be not a circle, but a line." In other words, there is no value in ruminating about past misdeeds, over and over remembering, analyzing, and feeling guilty; but there is value in putting the past behind and pressing steadily forward to the accomplishment of the new goal of becoming a true server.

The third paragraph lists a series of intuitive lessons, also from the soul, that describe how to prepare the personality for a life of service ("Prepare the form"). First, "let the eyes look forward, not on either side." In other words, be occupied with taking the next step in service, without any desire to gain the fruits from earlier steps. Wise servers work to their utmost ability. Then, having done their part, they pass on to continue their work, without experiencing pride over what they have done or depression because of any lack of accomplishment. They do not care if the result is different from what they anticipated, provided that they faithfully did the highest thing they knew. They do not care that they receive criticism from others, provided that the inner self remains calm and non-accusing. And they do not care if there seems to be little to show for their labors, provided that their inner light increases.[5]

Second, "let the ears be closed to all the outer voices." Irrespective of the opinions of the world's experts, disciples must have the courage to depend on themselves and on the conclusions they themselves have come to during moments of illumination. When running counter to public opinion, they have to do the right thing as they see and know it: speaking the words told by the inner voice of the soul and acting in detail according to how the inner self urges.[6]

Third, have "the hands clenched, the body braced, and mind alert." These symbols are descriptive of someone who is preparing for a fight, such as a boxing match. Their meaning is that a disciple must overcome any cowardice and be prepared to face vigorous opposition. Cowardice may be the quality that produces the greatest number of failures among those who seek adeptship. Almost without realizing it, people run away from difficulty, from inharmonious conditions, from places that involve problems, and from circumstances that call for action of a high sort. This lesson of overcoming cowardice is especially appropriate for disciples on the first ray because their peculiar nature is to act as a destroyer. In the past, they used destructive forces to achieve their own self-centered ambitions. But now they are being prepared to become agents of destruction under the divine plan, which means destroying old crystallized patterns that are no longer appropriate for modern times. However, there will always be people who wish to preserve the old patterns, the old ways of doing things, and they will present vigorous opposition. Instead of fleeing from these difficult circumstances, the disciple must learn to stay in them and by so doing live a life that is an example to others.[7]

Fourth, "emotion is not used in furthering of the Plan." The preceding lessons require the elimination of several types of glamours or emotional distortions. After freeing themselves from those glamours, disciples can discern a subtler class of distortions, sometimes called "the glamours of the Path," which are present when they take pride in treading the spiritual path or furthering the divine plan. For first-ray disciples, these distortions include the glamour of personal potency, the glamour of the Messiah complex in the field of politics, the glamour of selfish destiny, and the glamour of destruction. Because these glamours hinder progress and spoil service to others, they should be discovered and eliminated. Chapter 3 describes a systematic technique for accomplishing this emotional purification.[8]

And fifth, "love takes its place." The word *love* can be defined as a sense of identification with others. A gradual expansion of the capacity to love occurs by passing through the stages of love of mate, love of family, love of surrounding associates, love of country, and then love of humanity. It is important for servers on the first ray to keep on expanding their awareness until that final identification is achieved. The approach is to see humanity as a single whole and then identify with that whole, to think of the human kingdom of nature as a single organism and then feel and know oneself to be part of

that organism. In this way, separative awareness can be super-
seded by the consciousness of the larger and wider whole.[9]

Meditation can be defined as deliberately evoking a quality
associated with a state of consciousness higher than one's normal state, with the effect of increasing the activity of a chakra
not yet developed. This definition implies that our approach to
meditation will change as we progress on the spiritual path. For
instance, for an aspirant on the probationary path, one method
of meditation is deliberately applying new virtues. Because
each new virtue is an aspect of group consciousness, this meditation activates the heart chakra. After the first initiation is
attained, an effective meditation is expressing the creativity of
an illumined mind, which increases the activity of the throat
chakra. After the second initiation is attained, an effective
meditation is temporarily becoming polarized in the realm of
abstract thought or the soul. This last type of meditation is
sometimes called "occult meditation," and it increases the activity of the brow chakra.

Disciples who have succeeded in following the earlier lessons attain the second initiation and become ready to practice
the method of occult meditation appropriate for the first ray.
The final paragraph of the technique gives a description of
someone who is carrying out this method of meditation, as seen
from the vantage point of an observer who is both clairvoyant
and telepathic. A clairvoyant is able to perceive symbols representing the inner state of consciousness of the one being
observed. Here, a clairvoyant is able to see that "the symbol of
a moving point of light appears above the brow." This symbol
shows that the disciple is actively utilizing the brow chakra,
indicating temporary polarization in the soul while the mind is
quiescent. Afterward the mind becomes active, and a telepathic observer is able to register the following sequence of
thought ("The keynote of the life though uttered not, yet still is
clearly heard"). First, "I move to power," meaning that the
disciple's mind is illumined and moves with divine purpose.
Next, "I am the One," meaning that the person sees humanity

as a single whole and identifies with that whole. Next, "we are a Unity in power," meaning that the creative imagination is used to develop methods of cooperation with other servers. And finally, "all is for the power and glory of the One," meaning that the disciple's life is inspired by the desire to serve and uplift humanity.[10]

Occult meditation is different from the typical service and cooperation of an aspirant on the probationary path — such service and cooperation are based on a theory, with a determination to prove the value of that theory. Rather, the effort here is to merge consciously with the soul, even if only temporarily. Because it is the soul that decides, plans, and works, there is spontaneous illumination, creativity, and inspiration.

The Sanskrit word *karma* means action, and karma yoga refers to the path of dedicated action. The approach in this yoga is to renounce all egotistical goals for one's activities. Through this renunciation, one becomes sensitive to the divine will and is able to leave the choice and direction of one's activities to that will. Sri Krishna in *The Bhagavad Gita* describes the method of karma yoga as follows: "To work, alone, you are entitled, never to its fruit. Neither let your motive be the fruit of action, nor let your attachment be to non-action. Being established in yoga . . . perform your actions, casting off attachment and remaining even-minded both in success and in failure."[11] Karma yoga is similar to the first-ray technique because both emphasize working to promote human welfare in a spirit of nonattachment.

Ray Two

"Again I stand; a point within a circle and yet myself."

The love of love must dominate, not love of being loved. The power to draw unto oneself must dominate, but into the worlds of form that power must some day fail to penetrate. This is the first step towards a deeper search.

The word goes forth from soul to form: "Release thyself from all that stands around, for it has naught for thee, so look to me. I am the One who builds, sustains and draws thee on and up. Look unto me with eyes of love, and seek the path which leads from the outer circle to the point.

"I, at the point, sustain. I, at the point, attract. I, at the point, direct and choose and dominate. I, at the point, love all, drawing them to the centre and moving forward with the travelling points towards that great Centre where the One Point stands." What mean you by that *Word*?[12]

The second ray is called the ray of love-wisdom. During the stage of selfish influence, second-ray individuals long for material comfort and well-being, and they subordinate all of their available soul powers for achieving those ends. They have a great need of receiving love from others, and they try to secure that love by emotionally manipulating those they consider necessary for their comfort.

Each technique of integration has a basic theme that runs through its various paragraphs. In the case of the second-ray technique, that theme is love and the various stages of love. However, for most people, love is not really love but a mixture of a desire to love and a desire to be loved, plus a willingness to do anything to show and evoke this feeling. This pseudo-love is often the basis of many human relationships, such as between husband and wife, parents and children. People who desire this pseudo-love can be extremely selfish. These people do not know the love of the soul that is free and that leaves others to be free. Instead, they try to obligate and imprison those they desire to serve, to draw forth affection in return and improve their own self-esteem. This effort to obligate is really a form of anger and leads to conflict, guilt, and bitterness.[13]

Second-ray individuals experience the crisis of evocation in the following way. They intuitively sense the basic quality of the soul, which is inclusive love, and then contrast this quality with the anger, hatred, and bitterness of their interpersonal relationships. Since the old way of relating with people resulted in disappointment, they wonder whether there is a better way and how they might find that way. They begin to seek answers by closely studying from various books, teachers, and teachings, which provide an outer confirmation for their own evolving understanding.

The following definitions may be helpful when interpreting the second-ray technique. The word *alignment* refers to bringing the integrated aspects of a human being into line with the next higher aspect to be integrated. During each stage of the spiritual path, we learn to increase our alignment in a manner suitable for that stage. In esoteric philosophy, the *ring-pass-not* refers to the circle of the individual's influence, or the boundary of the field of activity for the central life force. This boundary is determined by limitations of circumstance, sometimes called karma in Eastern philosophy, and by the individual's own sense of separateness.

In the first paragraph, the word *stand* refers to increasing alignment; *circle*, to the individual's ring-pass-not; and *point* within the circle, to the center of one's being, which is the soul. As indicated by this paragraph, the aspirant's first step on the path of probation is to increase his alignment, so that he can observe from the vantage point of the soul everything included within his ring-pass-not. The light of self-observation then reveals himself as he is, or as the soul sees the personality. In particular, he sees that he generally approaches his interpersonal relationships with the motive of gratifying his own need of being loved.

The second paragraph of the technique describes the next step on the path of probation. Through a careful process of reasoning, second-ray aspirants come to the following conclusions. To have right relationships with others, referring to relationships that are free of conflict and manipulation, "the love of love must dominate, not love of being loved." In other words, they must have concern regarding the welfare of everyone involved in a relationship, rather than with just gratifying their own need of being loved. In the past they tried to hold onto people to avoid losing their affection, because of doubts about whether they could find others who would take their place. Now they want to express true or inclusive love, because such love would enable them to become more attractive and capable of drawing satisfying relationships to themselves ("The power to draw unto oneself must dominate"). They sense that true love already exists within themselves, because it is the basic quality of the soul, but that inner barriers can prevent this love from penetrating their mental, emotional, and physical worlds of experience ("but into the worlds of form that power must some day fail to penetrate"). For instance, they may see that they have such characteristic vices as indifference to others, coldness, contempt towards others, and over-absorption in study. Arriving at these intellectual conclusions is only a "first step towards a deeper search." It is necessary to take a further step by learning to express new virtues, such as unselfishness, love, compassion, and tangible service.

When their lives have been successfully reoriented, disciples complete the probationary path and attain the first initiation. As outlined in the third paragraph of Bailey's technique, they receive intuitively from the soul a series of lessons that describe what must be done next. The first lesson is to "release thyself from all that stands around." The word *all* indicates that second-ray disciples tend to be responsive to all glamours that stand around the emotional plane, rather than to only a few. However, their characteristic glamours include the glamour of the love of being loved, the glamour of personal wisdom, the glamour of selfish responsibility, the glamour of self-pity, and the glamour of selfish service. Second-ray disciples are often fully aware of the particular glamour to which they are responding. If they think of this responsiveness as a sin or a failure, a negative attitude of inferiority and distress will develop, delaying their release. They are able to gain release by carefully scrutinizing that glamour until there is a realization of its essential illusionary nature ("it has naught for thee").[14]

At this point in their integration, disciples identify with the personality but understand that they have a soul. The second lesson is to look to the soul ("so look to me") for building and sustaining all activities and for the guidance needed to advance spiritually ("I am the One who builds, sustains and draws thee on and up"). Because the guidance of the soul can be thought of as being the inner voice of God, this lesson is sometimes called "practicing the presence of God." To accomplish this lesson, disciples need to train themselves in spiritual discrimination and gain the ability to distinguish between instinct and intuition, lower and higher mind, desire and spiritual impulse, and selfish aspiration and divine incentive.[15]

While practicing the presence of God is a desirable and needed step, it is often practiced with a sense of duality. For instance, there may be a sense of separation between the lower mind and the indwelling soul, between the little self and the real Self, or between the human life expression and the spiritual life expression. The third lesson is to look upon the soul "with eyes of love." Because the word *love* refers to an intuitive understanding of the essential unity between the perceiver and the perceived, this phrase implies the following injunctions: Think of the soul as being the inner self, rather than something that is separate and apart; think of oneself and others as being souls, rather than limited human beings; and, as far as possible, steadily change any sense of duality into a sense of identification with the soul.[16]

And the fourth lesson is to "seek the path which leads from the outer circle to the point." Although second-ray disciples are instructed to seek the path leading to integration of personality with soul, there is no one who can define that path for them. They have already submitted to many guides, only to find them to be blind leaders of the blind. They have already tried many organized teachings, only to find them all lacking. Nothing is left except becoming one's own guide and finding the way *alone*. This aloneness is not due to any sense of separateness the disciple might have but is due to the nature of the spiritual path itself. Through clear perception, following the guidance of the soul, and right identification, one has to construct one's own path, just as the spider spins its web out of the center of its being.[17]

A disciple who has succeeded in carrying out the foregoing instructions attains the second initiation and becomes ready for the final stage in the integration process. As indicated in the fourth paragraph, the discipline now is to increase alignment still further by consciously achieving a state of fusion with the soul ("I, at the point"), while holding the mental body steady in the light of the soul. Through this practice, one can "sustain" material affairs with wisdom; have right relationships with others and "attract" their friendships in return; "direct" one's mental thinking, "choose" one's emotional responses, and "dominate" one's physical body.

This discipline enables   true love and wisdom to be expressed ("I, at the point, love all"), where the latter can be defined as love revealing itself through service. True love is not the sentimental conception that is often discussed: it is not the love that sees no faults or limitations in others; it is not the love that seeks not to correct others; and it is not the love that recognizes no differences in points of development in others. True love sees with clarity the deficiencies of any form and seeks to render appropriate aid to the indwelling life; it wisely discriminates between those who need help and those who do not need attention; it hears with precision and understands the inner thoughts of others; and it seeks to blend the workers of the world into one unified whole.[18]

After developing the ability of raising consciousness to a point of soul fusion, even if only temporarily, the disciple is ready to practice the method of occult meditation that is appropriate for the second ray. As mentioned in the Introduction, a human being is actually a trinity consisting of personality, soul, and spirit. The spiritual mind, discussed in chapter 1, is included as an aspect of the spirit. While the personality on the physical plane is a vehicle for the manifestation of the soul, the soul is the vehicle on a higher plane for the manifestation of the spirit. Occult meditation for the second ray consists of making definite and sustained effort to sense the spirit, or the presence, in all forms. This meditation is sometimes called "the Technique of the Presence," and it is described by Bailey as "the effort to isolate the germ or seed of divinity which has brought all forms into being."[19] This meditation is not concerned with attaining a loving attitude toward all people and circumstances — that was the effort during the probationary period before the first initiation. Nor is it concerned with living with a sense of the guiding presence of God — that was the effort between the first and second initiations. Rather, the effort here is first using the light of the soul to perceive in every form the vision of the soul ("drawing them to the centre") and then using that light to move even further behind, revealing intuitively the inner spirit where God Immanent is present ("and moving forward with the travelling points towards that great Centre where the One Point stands").

This meditation helps the disciple to unfold the intuition, dispel illusions, reveal the soul, and indicate the presence. It also opens up the world of intuitive divine ideas. Bailey's technique ends with the following question: "What mean you by that Word?" Here "Word" refers to some intuitive idea that is sensed during the meditation process. By pondering over, understanding, and then applying those ideas in daily life, the disciple becomes prepared to take the third initiation.[20]

A Course in Miracles is an example of a teaching that incorporates the initial stages of the second-ray technique: understanding interpersonal relationships, expressing new virtues such as love and forgiveness, and releasing oneself from various emotional distortions. Groups that study *A Course in Miracles* typically begin their meetings with the following invocation:

I am here only to be truly helpful.
I am here to represent Him Who sent me.
I do not have to worry about what to say or what to
    do, because He Who sent me will direct me.
I am content to be wherever He wishes, knowing He
    goes there with me.
I will be healed as I let Him teach me to heal.[21]

This invocation illustrates what is called "practicing the presence of God."

The Sanskrit word *jnana* means wisdom. Jnana yoga, the path of wisdom, is an example of a teaching that incorporates the later stages of the second-ray technique. The first step in this yoga is practicing self-discipline and purification, which develops a longing for freedom and the ability to understand deep truths. The second step is intellectual reflection upon the nature of the inner spiritual self, that which is neither mutable nor perishable. The third step is right discrimination: rejecting identification with whatever is transitory, including the personality and the phenomenal world, and instead becoming identified with the spiritual self. The fourth step is employing meditation to attain the non-dual realization of the spiritual self, not only in one's own being but in all beings. And the final step is realizing that the phenomenal world is not separate from divine consciousness and has an important role to play in human evolution.[22]

Ray Three

"Pulling the threads of Life, I stand, enmeshed within my self-created glamour. Surrounded am I by the fabric I have woven. I see naught else.

"*The love of truth* must dominate, not love of my own thoughts, or love of my ideas or forms; love of the

ordered process must control, not love of my own
wild activity."

The word goes forth from soul to form: "Be still.
Learn to stand silent, quiet and unafraid. I, at the
centre, *Am*. Look up along the line and not along the
many lines which, in the space of aeons, you have
woven. These hold thee prisoner. Be still. Rush not
from point to point, nor be deluded by the outer
forms and that which disappears. Behind the forms,
the Weaver stands and silently he weaves."[23]

The third ray is that of activity and adaptability. During
the stage of selfish influence, persons on this ray are involved
in intense material and mental activity but with the wrong
motive. They spend their time and energy manipulating, planning, and arranging but manage to get nowhere. They are
always occupied with distant goals but fail to achieve the immediate objective. Because changes in circumstances frustrate
their carefully laid plans, they experience futility.

Due to their efforts to achieve success in the world, third-
ray individuals attain sufficient alignment with the soul to
sense the creativity of their inner nature. After contrasting that
creativity with the relative uselessness of their outer lives, they
undergo the crisis of evocation and become ready to take the
initial step on the spiritual path.

The first paragraph of the Bailey's technique describes the
initial step of self-observation. While manipulating the material world ("Pulling the threads of Life"), aspirants increase
their alignment ("I stand") to observe their underlying motivations. Through this process, they see that they have become
enmeshed within a glamour, referring to a mental illusion that
has been intensified with desire ("enmeshed within my self-
created glamour"). They realize that this glamour is like a
fabric that completely surrounds them and that they have
woven it out of their dreams and longings for a future glory
("Surrounded am I by the fabric I have woven"). Owing to this

glamour, they are unable to see their circumstances without distortion ("I see naught else").

As shown by the second paragraph of the technique, the next step for aspirants is to think deeply about their situation and come to the following conclusion: To be free of illusions, "the love of truth must dominate," rather than the love of one's own thoughts, ideas, and plans. In other words, *what* is correct must be more important than *who* is correct. Because their characteristic vices include intellectual pride, coldness, and excessive criticism of others, they begin making the effort to display the opposite qualities: devotion to truth, sympathy, and tolerance. They also come to another conclusion: To be free of glamours, "love of the ordered process must control," which means that the desire to be efficient and accurate must be paramount. But if they allow themselves to be distracted by a desire for some prideful activity ("not love of my own wild activity"), then both time and energy would be wasted. Because their characteristic vices also include absentmindedness, inaccuracy in details, and uncoordinated activity, they begin displaying common sense, accuracy, and one-pointedness.

When this process of reorientation has been satisfactorily completed, the first initiation is attained. Because of their desire for illumination, third-ray disciples receive a series of lessons from the soul that are described in the final paragraph. The first lesson is to "be still," but this stillness does not mean that thoughts, feelings, and activities should be suppressed. Rather, it means learning to increase alignment even further ("Learn to stand") so that the earlier practice of self-observation can be deepened and prolonged. The approach is to become focused at a point of self-observation, which is the vantage point of the soul, and then observe the personality from that center. The resulting stillness is similar to what is present at the center of a storm or a whirlpool, enabling the activities of the personality to be observed without self-justification, self-criticism, or resistance ("silent, quiet and unafraid"). Because this observant attitude is difficult to maintain, chapter 3 describes several meditation exercises that may be helpful.

Second, become disentangled from unwise physical activities. This divine idleness can be achieved in the following manner: remain focused at the center of self-observation ("I, at the centre, Am"); have a clear and single-minded awareness of what is actually happening both inside and outside during the current moment ("Look up along the line"); and then respond to those opportunities that are already present. This process is quite different from trying to make new opportunities for oneself by looking "along the many lines" of thought leading into the future. In the past, third-ray disciples imagined that those lines of thought led to glory. However, over a period of time, those lines formed a veil of glamour ("which, in the space of aeons, you have woven"), and now that veil imprisons them ("These hold thee prisoner"). By cultivating insight and a fluid response to the immediate need, rather than a sensitive reaction to a distant goal, they can transform themselves into persons of practical action on behalf of humanity.[24]

Third, become disentangled from emotional distortions. This release is difficult to achieve because it involves the loss of some false pride. The necessary approach is to use the mind to examine a specific glamour while being still in the sense of maintaining the center of self-observation ("Be still"). Having such a center enables the inquiry of the mind to be guided by the wisdom of the soul, and it also enables any mental resistance and defensiveness regarding the glamour to be observed and eliminated. Through the determined facing of facts and the stern recognition of truth, the glamour can then be seen for what it essentially is and thus be made to disappear. By using this approach, third-ray disciples can overcome the glamours that have caused them to act in uncoordinated and inefficient ways ("Rush not from point to point"). For instance, their characteristic glamours include the glamour of being busy, the glamour of creative work, the glamour of active scheming, the glamour of devious manipulations, and the glamour of self-importance through knowledge and efficiency.[25]

And fourth, become disentangled from mental illusions. Here, it is necessary to achieve another type of stillness: a quiescent mind, yet one that is poised and alert, which is a stillness similar to that of a quiet millpond. After achieving that stillness, the mind can receive intuitive ideas from the soul. When the new understanding replaces the delusions of the rationalizing mind, there can be clear comprehension about the activities of body, speech, and mind ("nor be deluded by the outer forms") and about the phenomenal world ("and that which disappears").

The preceding discussion illustrates the following point: to resolve a problem on a lower level, it is necessary to rise to a higher level. Disentanglement from unwise physical activities occurs by ensuring that the emotional body has the proper motives, as selected using the discriminative power of the mind; disentanglement from emotional distortions occurs by using the mind to present information and facts, as guided by the wisdom of the soul; and disentanglement from mental distortions occurs by receiving the wisdom of the soul, which in turn is guided by insights from the spiritual mind.

When there has been success in this discipline of stillness, the disciple attains the second initiation and becomes ready to practice the method of occult meditation that is appropriate for the third ray. This meditation is indicated by the final sentence in the technique, where the word "Weaver" refers to the soul. The approach is to become focused behind the physical, emotional, and mental bodies ("Behind the forms"), merge consciously with the soul ("the Weaver stands"), and then allow the intrinsic nature of the soul to act ("and silently he weaves"). In the case of the third ray of activity, that intrinsic nature can be characterized as weaving, which means accumulating needed information, qualities, and materials, and then systematically adapting those factors in the service of humanity.[26]

It may be helpful to compare the first three Techniques of Integration. The first-ray technique emphasizes the value of becoming more inclusive, which means becoming identified with humanity as a whole. The second-ray technique emphasizes the value of looking to the soul for guidance and becoming identified with the soul. And the third-ray technique emphasizes the value of observing the personality without distortion. Owing to these differences, the approach to meditation that one is intuitively guided to follow will vary depending upon one's ray, as well as one's point of evolution along the spiritual path.

The third-ray technique is similar in several respects to Theravada Buddhism. This branch of Buddhism is considered to be an agnostic religion because it has virtually no mention of God, the soul, or the spiritual dimension of life. Rather, its emphasis is on achieving what are called "bare attention" and "clear comprehension." Bare attention is the clear and single-minded awareness of what is actually happening to oneself during the immediate moment, both inside and outside. This attention is called "bare" because it attends to just the bare facts of the perception without any reaction or judgment. Bare attention can then lead to clear comprehension. The Buddhist tradition distinguishes four kinds of clear comprehension: clear comprehension of purpose, which requires questioning whether an intended activity is in accordance with one's purpose or ideals; clear comprehension of suitability, which requires questioning whether the means or procedures chosen for a particular activity are suitable; clear comprehension of the domain of meditation, which means understanding that the earlier efforts should be extended to all activities of the body, speech, and mind; and clear comprehension of reality, which means being able to carry out the earlier efforts without any delusions.[27]

Ray Four

"Midway I stand between the forces which oppose each other. Longing am I for harmony and peace, and for the beauty which results from unity. I see the two. I see naught else but forces ranged opposing, and I, the one, who stands within the circle at the centre. Peace I demand. My mind is bent upon it. Oneness with all I seek, yet form divides. War upon every side I find, and separation. Alone I stand and am. I know too much."

The love of unity must dominate, and love of peace and harmony. Yet not that love, based on a longing for relief, for peace to self, for unity because it carries with it that which is pleasantness.

The word goes forth from soul to form. "Both sides are one. There is no war, no difference and no isolation. The warring forces seem to war from the point at which you stand. Move on a pace. See truly with the opened eye of inner vision and you will find, not two but one; not war but peace; not isolation but a heart which rests upon the centre. Thus shall the beauty of the Lord shine forth. The hour is now." [28]

The fourth ray is that of harmony through conflict. During the stage of selfish influence, fourth-ray individuals feel identified with all humanity. Being unable to reconcile their own needs with those of others, they feel torn by a series of dilemmas and think of each dilemma as a choice between a higher way and a lower way regarding some issue. After arming themselves with various defense mechanisms, they choose the alternative that can be more easily justified.

The foregoing dilemmas occurred because the individuals applied the intuitive perception of the soul to their outer conditions. By applying the intuitive perception of the soul to their own inner struggles, they undergo the crisis of evocation and begin the path of probation.

The initial effort on the path of probation is self-observation, which is described in the technique's first paragraph. After detaching themselves from both alternatives of a particular dilemma ("Midway"), aspirants increase their alignment ("I stand") and become aware of their underlying motivations. They see that they are torn between contradictory feelings regarding the two alternatives ("between the forces which oppose each other"). They also observe a longing to express the basic quality of the soul, which is harmony and peace, and to express the basic technique, which is achieving synthesis by unifying opposing forces ("Longing am I for harmony and peace, and for the beauty which results from unity"). Due to the clarity gained by observing these motivations, they realize that they have only two basic options ("I see the two"). Either they can resume struggling with the dilemma, use their defense mechanisms, and then pick any one of the two alternatives. Or they can relinquish the struggle, apply a process of conflict resolution, and then see what happens. They recognize that choosing the first option always results in an unsatisfactory outcome. On the other hand, they are not sure that choosing the second option will be better, but they feel a favorable outcome is at least possible. During the stage of selfish influence, they always chose the first option. But after reaching the path of probation, they increasingly choose the second one.

Through careful reasoning and experiment, fourth-ray aspirants eventually discover a systematic process for resolving any particular dilemma. As outlined in the final portion of the first paragraph, this process has the following steps. First, study the alternatives of the dilemma, while being aligned with the soul and detached from both alternatives. More specifically, think of the two alternatives as being arranged on opposite sides of a circle, while thinking of oneself as standing at the center of the circle ("I see naught else but forces ranged opposing, and I, the one, who stands within the circle at the centre"). Second, be determined to find a satisfactory solution, which means having the will to victory ("Peace I demand"). Third, apply the concrete mind in an intense way, which requires bending every mental quality and controlling the lower nature ("My mind is bent on it"). Fourth, seek to understand the essence of both alternatives, and why each alternative excludes the other ("Oneness with all I seek, yet form divides"). Fifth, observe the conflicting emotional reactions to each alternative, as well as the feeling of isolation due to being detached from both alternatives ("War upon every side I find, and separation"). Sixth, in spite of any sense of despairing futility, be steadfast in maintaining alignment with the soul and detachment from both alternatives ("Alone I stand and am"). And seventh, recognize the activity of the soul within, which can now begin to do its work through the illumination of the mind ("I know too much").

The sixth step in the above list is crucial and requires some additional explanation. For this method of conflict resolution to be successful, the personality must remain in alignment with the soul. However, alignment is a gradual and progressive process. During the path of probation, maintaining alignment refers simply to having the right motive. As indicated by the second paragraph of the technique, "the love of unity must dominate" the inquiry, which is a desire to achieve peace and harmony for everyone involved in a dispute ("love of peace and harmony"). This love of unity is not the same as a longing for personal relief, for peace and harmony to the self, or for circumstances that are more pleasant ("Yet not that love, based on a longing for relief, for peace to self, for unity because it carries with it that which is pleasantness"). If one allows oneself to be motivated by these self-centered considerations, then no satisfactory resolution can be found.

Through their self-observation, fourth-ray aspirants discover several impediments hindering their ability to implement the above list of steps. These impediments include self-centeredness, lack of moral courage, inaccuracy, indolence, worrying, and strong passions. To carry out those steps, they must reorient their lives by deliberately acquiring the opposite qualities, such as unselfishness, confidence, accuracy, self-control, mental balance, and serenity. When this reorientation is successfully completed, they attain the first initiation.

The third paragraph of the technique corresponds to the path of discipleship. By making additional efforts to resolve inner conflicts, the disciple is able to evoke from the soul some deeper lessons regarding this subject. First, "both sides are one," meaning that the two conflicting alternatives in a dilemma are part of a single glamorous condition. While immersed within this glamour of the pair of opposites, the disciple swings back and forth between different feelings. These feelings can run the gamut from joyfulness, as one seeks to identify with the object of aspiration, to the blackest despair if one fails to do so. Although the disciple may think of this inner struggle as being a conflict between personality and soul, the struggle is entirely emotional in nature and is not of the soul at all.[29]

Second, each alternative in a dilemma has the following structure: There is a position or conclusion that was accepted in the past but that may not be appropriate for the present context; under each position is a specific glamour or emotional distortion; and under each glamour is an essential interest. The position is an illusion that has been brought down to the emotional plane, where it is clothed by the associated glamour. This unification of illusion and glamour constitutes a double problem that hinders the clear perception of the essential interest. Although there is conflict on the level of positions, "there is no war, no difference and no isolation" on the deeper level of essential interests because these interests are in harmony with one another. Thus, the dilemma seems to exist only because of the way it is being perceived ("The warring forces seem to war from the point at which you stand").

For instance, suppose that the dilemma is choosing between selflessness, such as donating wealth to the poor, and selfishness, such as enjoying possessions. Perhaps under the seeming selflessness is the glamour of conflict, referring to the desire of imposing righteousness and peace on others, and under that is an essential interest in assisting others. Perhaps under the selfishness is the glamour of harmony, referring to the desire for personal comfort and satisfaction, and under that is an essential interest in satisfying vital personal needs. Although the two positions are conflicting, the two essential interests can be satisfied in a harmonious way.

Third, the perception of the dilemma can be changed by moving from the world of feeling to the world of the illumined mind ("Move on a pace"), which requires a further increase in alignment with the soul. In particular, it is necessary to subject the conflicting alternatives to a careful scrutiny using the mind, while the mind is guided and controlled by the opened eye of the soul ("See truly with the opened eye of inner vision").

And fourth, through the above process, it will be found that the inner conflict has been resolved. There is no longer a choice between alternative positions but a clear understanding of what to do ("you will find, not two but one"). There is no longer a struggle between contradictory glamours but an inner harmony among the essential interests ("not war but peace"). And there is no longer a feeling of separation between different parts of the self but an inner unity based on taking the middle path between the pair of opposites ("not isolation but a heart which rests upon the centre").

When there has been success in resolving the emotional conflicts that occur within, the disciple attains the second initiation and becomes ready to practice the method of occult meditation that is appropriate for the fourth ray. This method has the following steps: increase alignment still further and become temporarily polarized in the soul; have a realization of the inner harmony and unity that exists among human beings; and then work to resolve external conflicts, thereby enabling that harmony and unity to manifest outwardly ("Thus shall the beauty of the Lord shine forth").

All of the earlier lessons are now applicable to working in this larger context, as discussed next. When a conflict occurs between two groups of people, these groups are actually emotionally tied together to form a single interacting dynamic system ("Both sides are one"), such as a family, community, or nation. Although their positions may be in conflict, their essential interests are in harmony because their souls are in harmony ("There is no war, no difference and no isolation"). These groups are in conflict because of the way they are perceiving their interests ("The warring forces seem to war from the point at which you stand"). The disciple can help resolve this conflict by assisting the two sides to shift their perceptions, which can be done by guiding them from the world of feeling to the world of the illumined mind ("Move on a pace"). The actual resolution would be in the form of an agreement that synthesizes the essential interests of both sides ("not two but one"), thereby revealing the underlying harmony and unity that were always present ("not war but peace"). The technique ends with the phrase "the hour is now." Achieving the needed shifts in perception does not require a duration of time but can happen immediately.

In summary, the third paragraph of the fourth-ray technique is written in such a way that it could refer to the resolution of either an inner or an outer struggle. Because the essential concerns of both sides in the conflict are met, this resolution is in the form of a triple victory: a victory of the two sides plus the one who is at the center, where the latter refers to the soul in the case of an inner struggle and to the mediating disciple in the case of an outer struggle.

Some of the ideas in the Technique of Integration for the fourth ray can be found in a relatively new branch of social science called conflict resolution. In this social science, conflict is accepted as a natural and sometimes even desirable component of human nature. The emphasis is on improving the process of resolution, so that conflicts can be ameliorated through negotiation and mediation rather than through physical force. The approach is to focus on the underlying interests of the parties in a conflict, rather than on their overtly stated positions. The goal is to negotiate what is called an "integrative agreement," which is a reconciliation or integration of the underlying interests. Such an agreement should be contrasted with a compromise that is reached when the parties make concessions and that produces a lower joint benefit. By negotiating an integrative agreement, each party can be a winner, which is important because a loser may ultimately retaliate.[30]

It may be helpful to give a concrete illustration of the foregoing approach. There are at present two different groups in the United States that are involved in the national security debate: liberal "doves," who are working for peace through disarmament, and conservative "hawks," who are working for peace through strength. Although members of both groups are seeking to avoid war and increase the security of their country, they are driven by entirely different fears and beliefs. Each group is characterized by an antagonistic orientation: The doves blame the military-industrial complex of the United States for the arms race, while the hawks blame the leaders of the Soviet Union. Opposition exists between these groups on the level of overtly stated positions: The doves advocate disarmament to decrease the likelihood of a war, while the hawks advocate increasing military power to avoid being coerced by the Soviet Union.

Because of these conflicting positions, only one group can be dominant at a time, leaving the other group feeling insecure and yearning to get its own way. Nevertheless, common ground can be found on the deeper level of fundamental interests: Both groups are interested in preventing war and preserving the democratic heritage of the United States. Thus, there exists the possibility of forging a consensus that would satisfy the concerns of both groups without requiring any compromise. In particular, there might be a consensus for a mutual and verifiable reduction in offensive weapons, coupled with the deployment of strictly defensive weapons. For instance, anti-tank weapons could be deployed instead of tanks, or anti-aircraft weapons instead of bomber aircraft. The point is that the United States can improve its security by deploying defensive weapons, but without threatening the security of the Soviet Union. Deploying these weapons would not continue the arms race, because the Soviet Union would not need to acquire additional weapons to defend itself. For such a consensus to occur, it is necessary for both doves and hawks to perceive their conflict in a fresh way, which requires that these groups develop an attitude of mutual respect and a willingness to listen to each other.[31]

Ray Five

"Towards me I draw the garment of my God. I see and know His form. I take that garment, piece by piece. I know its shape and colour, its form and type, its parts component and its purposes and use. I stand amazed, I see naught else. I penetrate the mysteries of form, but not the *Mystery*. I see the garment of my God. I see naught else."

Love of the form is good but only as the form is known for what it is — the veiling vase of life. Love of the form must never hide the Life which has its place behind, the *One* who brought the form into the light of day, and preserves it for His use, — The *One* Who lives, and loves and serves the form, the One Who *Is*.

The Word goes forth from soul to form: "Behind that form, I am. Know Me. Cherish and know and understand the nature of the veils of life, but know as well the One Who lives. Know Me. Let not the forms of nature, their processes and powers prevent thy searching for the Mystery which brought the mysteries to thee. Know well the form, but leave it joyously and search for Me.

"Detach thy thought from form and find Me waiting underneath the veils, the many-sided shapes, the glamours and the thought-forms which hide my real Self. Be not deceived. Find Me. Know Me. Then use the forms which then will neither veil nor hide the Self, but will permit the nature of that Self to penetrate the veils of life, revealing all the radiance of God, His power and magnetism; revealing all there is of form, of life, of beauty and usefulness. The mind reveals the *One*. The mind can blend and fuse the form and life. Thou art the One. Thou art the form. Thou art the mind. Know this."[32]

The fifth ray is the ray of concrete knowledge, or science. Individuals on this ray have a thirst for knowledge and are by nature scientific researchers. Either as vocation or avocation, they find some problem to study. Their efforts are aimed at comprehending the meanings and relationships that lie beyond their present understanding. Thus, they are working toward what could be characterized as expansion, inclusion, and enlightenment.

In fact, the process of scientific research is similar to raja yoga, the path of mental discipline. This yoga is considered to be "kingly," which is the meaning of the Sanskrit word *raja*, because of the power and wisdom that are conferred. The initial stages of raja yoga are concentration, in which the effort is to remain focused on some seed thought and not be distracted by other issues; meditation, in which there is prolonged attention and creative thinking regarding the seed thought; and contemplation, in which the soul aspect is active and intuitively perceives the inner relationships underlying the seed thought.[33]

Researchers are actually practicing yoga, in the foregoing sense, when they focus thought on some issue in an attentive, prolonged, and inquiring way. This issue could be a problem from any department of human knowledge, including religion, science, economics, and so forth. To be an adequate researcher, one has to develop a strong will, capacity to endure, and patient persistence. These qualities enable one to achieve the first stage of the raja yoga process, which is concentration. To be a good researcher, one has to achieve the second stage, meditation, in order to think with clarity, eliminate incorrect formulations, and come to sound conclusions. To be a superior researcher, one has to achieve the third stage, contemplation, to formulate intuitively new hypotheses and investigate those hypotheses. The point is that research into any topic, when properly done, can lead to the coordination of the personality and later to the awakening of the intuition of the soul.[34]

The first paragraph of Bailey's symbolic technique describes the crisis of evocation for the fifth ray. Individuals undergoing this experience have been investigating material forms but not the life that animates those forms ("Towards me I draw the garment of my God"). Their investigations have been based on two key assumptions: empiricism, or the belief that sensory experience is the only valid source of knowledge ("I see and know His form"), and reductionism, or the belief that understanding is acquired by reducing phenomena to more elementary ones ("I take that garment, piece by piece"). With these assumptions, they have accumulated knowledge about material shapes and colors, about structures and relationships, and about the component parts and their interrelations and dependencies ("I know its shape and colour, its form and type, its parts component and its purposes and use"). However, this process of doing research has increased their alignment with the soul ("I stand"), awakening their inner understanding. Because they can now infer the existence of a nonmaterial life, they are "amazed" that something so important was left out of their theories. Not knowing how to investigate this nonmaterial life ("I see nought else"), they call on their inner understanding for guidance and begin the path of probation.

As described by the rest of the first paragraph, the first step for aspirants is to take stock of their lives. They recognize that they have penetrated the mysteries of the material world but not the mystery of life ("I penetrate the mysteries of form, but not the Mystery"). Remaining unanswered are such questions as What is life? What is energy? What is the nature of being? They also observe their underlying motivations: devotion to material forms and activity ("I see the garment of my God") without any appreciation of holistic or religious values ("I see naught else").

As outlined in the second paragraph of the technique, the next step is to arrive at the following conclusions. "Love of the form is good but only as the form is known for what it is — the veiling vase of life." The pursuit of knowledge about the material world, with empirical data and reductionistic explanations, must never hide the life that lies behind ("Love of the form must never hide the Life which has its place behind"). For proper balance, there must also be the pursuit of a second and complementary kind of knowledge that is concerned with teleology, or the idea that an overall design or purpose in nature has caused the phenomena in the material world and is directing that phenomena toward a definite end ("the One who brought the form into the light of day, and preserves it for His use"); holism, or the idea that a greater irreducible whole is responsible for life, love, and activity in the physical body ("The One Who lives, and loves and serves the form"); and mysticism, or the idea that ultimate reality can be directly apprehended ("the One Who Is").

Through their self-observation, fifth-ray aspirants discover certain habit patterns that hinder their ability to have proper balance and acquire the new kind of knowledge. For instance, these habit patterns may include narrowness, arrogance, prejudice, lack of sympathy, and lack of reverence. To detach themselves from the grip of material experiences, they begin to develop the opposite patterns, such as wide-mindedness, devotion, love, sympathy, and reverence. This reorientation requires mastery of the first stage of raja yoga, which is concentration, so that attention can be held on developing the new habit patterns.

After reorienting their lives and attaining the first initiation, fifth-ray disciples intuitively receive the lessons given in the third paragraph. First, behind the personality there exists the spiritual self ("Behind that form, I am"), and the time has come to gain knowledge about that inner self ("Know Me"). They should continue to study, know, and understand the various aspects of the personality ("Cherish and know and understand the nature of the veils of life"), but they are ready to take the further step of exploring the source of life ("but know as well the One Who lives"). During the path of probation, they wanted to learn about the nonmaterial world in general, but now they are being guided to narrow their inquiries and investigate esoteric psychology, which is the science of the soul ("Know Me").

Second, avoid being preoccupied with the "forms of nature, their processes and powers." Such a preoccupation would prevent an investigation of the deeper mystery of life, which is responsible for the mysteries of the material world ("prevent thy searching for the Mystery which brought the mysteries to thee"). Because fifth-ray disciples find satisfaction in the power of thought and have pride in their mental competence, their characteristic glamours are associated with concrete knowledge. For instance, these glamours include the glamour of materiality, the glamour of the intellect, the glamour of knowledge and of definition, and the glamour of assurance based on a narrow point of view. Because these glamours can lead to being preoccupied with the world of the concrete and intellectual, it is important to become free of them. The necessary approach requires mastery of the first two stages of raja yoga: concentration, consisting of holding the attention on a particular glamour; and meditation, consisting of using analysis, discrimination, and right thought to deal with that glamour.

And third, experience the contemplation stage of raja yoga through the study and interpretation of symbols. Contemplation is an activity of the soul while the mind is held in a state of quiescence. The first step is using concentration and meditation to analyze the form aspect of some chosen symbol or seed thought ("Know well the form"). This step is sometimes called "meditation with seed" and consists of reflecting on the nature of the form, the quality of the form, the purpose of the form, and the life animating the form. The second step is to leave the form ("but leave it") by entering a transition period of mental steadiness and waiting, which is sometimes called "meditation without seed" or "without an object." This period is no longer a process of thought but is not yet contemplation. It must be entered with the quality of emotional self-reliance ("joyously") so that the mind is positive, alert, and well-controlled, neither responsive to sensory impressions nor distracted by reverie. And the third step is discovering how to become polarized temporarily in the soul ("and search for Me"), which is the contemplation stage. After this new and higher state of awareness is experienced, there is understanding regarding the abstract intent of the symbol.[35]

Among the various rays, persons on the fifth ray suffer the least from glamour but are primarily the victims of illusion. By easily expressing the power of thought, they tend to think of themselves as self-sufficient. By being preoccupied with the concrete mind, they are apt to ignore and refuse to admit the existence of a spiritual dimension. And by being set in their ways, they have difficulty in recognizing what the mind is intended to reveal—the divine spiritual self. These conditions are different types of illusion, or ways that the concrete mind interposes itself and distorts perception. When the reality of the soul is experienced through the achievement of contemplation, these illusions become weaker and eventually disappear.[36]

After carrying out the above instructions, disciples attain the second initiation and become ready to practice the fifth-ray method of occult meditation. This method is described in a series of additional lessons given in the final paragraph of the technique. First, achieve the contemplation stage of raja yoga, which recapitulates some of the earlier training. After entering the transition period of meditation without seed or object ("Detach thy thought from form"), temporarily shift the polarization of consciousness into the soul ("and find Me waiting underneath the veils"), which requires piercing through that which hinders the downflow of higher knowledge: the physical restlessness, emotional glamours, and illusions on the concrete levels of the mental plane ("the many-sided shapes, the glamours and the thought-forms which hide my real Self"). Next, to avoid being deceived by illusions on the abstract levels of the mental plane ("Be not deceived"), temporarily shift the polarization into an even deeper aspect of the inner self, which is the spiritual mind ("Find Me"). After this higher alignment is established, the soul can receive insights from the spiritual mind that convey a direct knowledge of divinity ("Know Me"), and then the lower concrete mind can receive those insights from the soul.[37]

Second, enter the illumination stage of raja yoga. After becoming polarized once again in the mental body, formulate concrete thoughts and plans that embody the insights of the spiritual mind ("Then use the forms which then will neither veil nor hide the Self"). These thoughts and plans enable the nature of the spiritual mind to penetrate the illusions of the mental world ("but will permit the nature of that Self to penetrate the veils of life"), revealing the creative intelligence, purpose, and love of the spiritual dimension of life ("revealing all the radiance of God, His power and magnetism").

Third, enter the inspiration stage of raja yoga, which involves expressing the new understanding on the physical plane. This work may include presenting new discoveries regarding humanity and nature, conveying the spiritual ideas sensed in the life side of manifestation, bearing witness to the evolutionary plan that can be inferred from scientific laws, or making material improvements such as new inventions ("revealing all there is of form, of life, of beauty and usefulness").

And fourth, avoid the possibility of undue emphasis. Fifth-ray disciples may be so obsessed with their spiritual search that they become vague, impractical visionaries who fail to keep adequate contact with the material world. Or they may promote their new ideas and contributions in such an emotional way that fanaticism is produced. Thus, they have to ensure that the mind receives its share of illuminating energy from the soul ("The mind reveals the One") and that the mind then controls and integrates the physical and emotional bodies ("The mind can blend and fuse the form and life"). They are partly soul ("Thou art the One"), partly physical body ("Thou art the form"), and partly mind ("Thou art the mind"), and they must remember to keep all aspects of themselves in balance ("Know this").

Bailey has summarized the five stages of raja yoga as follows:

1. *Concentration*. This is the act of concentrating the mind, learning to focus it and so use it.

2. *Meditation*. The prolonged focusing of the attention in any direction and the steady holding of the mind on any desired idea.

3. *Contemplation*. An activity of the soul, detached from the mind, which is held in a state of quiescence.

4. *Illumination*. This is the result of the three preceding processes, and involves the carrying down into the brain of the knowledge achieved.

5. *Inspiration*. The result of illumination, as it demonstrates in the life of service.[38]

The Technique of Integration for the fifth ray involves applying one or more of these stages during each segment of the spiritual path.

Ray Six

"I see a vision. It satisfies desire; it feeds and stimulates its growth. I lay my life upon the altar of desire — the seen, the sensed, that which appeals to me, the satisfaction of my need — a need for that which is material, for that which feeds emotion, that satisfies the mind, that answers my demand for truth, for service, and my vision of the goal. It is the vision which I see, the dream I dream, the truth I hold, the active form which meets my need, that which I grasp and understand. *My* truth, *my* peace, *my* satisfied desire, *my* dream, *my* vision of reality, *my* limited ideal, *my* finite thought of God; — for these I struggle, fight and die."

Love of the truth must always be. Desire and aspiration, reaching out for that which is material or soaring upward towards the vision of reality must ever find their satisfaction. For this men work, driving themselves and irking others. They love the truth as they interpret it; they love the vision and the dream, forgetting that the truth is limited by mind — narrow and set, one-pointed, not inclusive; forgetting that the vision touches but the outer fringe of mystery, and veils and hides reality.

The word goes out from soul to form: "Run not so straight. The path that you are on leads to the outer circle of the life of God; the line goes forward to the outer rim. Stand at the centre. Look on every side. Die not for outer forms. Forget not God, Who dwells behind the vision. Love more your fellow men."[39]

The sixth ray is called the ray of devotion. During the stage of selfish influence, sixth-ray persons are able to sense some spiritual idea or higher intuitive value. They formulate the sensed idea into a particular vision, ideal, theology, doctrine, or dogma. Then they work to produce an expression of that vision, perhaps as devoted members of some religious, political, or social cause. However, they generally are fanatical and lack understanding of the viewpoints of others. Although professing a noble vision, they are shortsighted, suspicious, angry, and cruel. Because they overlook immediate opportunities and rush after some self-engendered vision of truth, their efforts are largely wasted.

After acknowledging the futility of their daily lives, sixth-ray persons undergo the crisis of evocation. Because of their basic nature, they have applied their desire and intelligence to manifest their formulated vision. They have tried all the approaches that seem to be possible but without success. Thus, they ask within themselves what they should do.

The first step on the probationary path is self-observation, and the thought pattern during this step is revealed in the first paragraph of Bailey's technique. Aspirants observe that they have formulated a mental concept of an underlying reality ("I see a vision") and that this concept satisfies their desire for importance and significance ("It satisfies desire"). Through their thoughts, feelings, and imagination, this concept feeds itself and stimulates its own growth ("It feeds and stimulates its growth"). They also observe that this concept is the product of a life based entirely on gratifying desire — for whatever is in the material and spiritual worlds that is appealing to them and satisfies their needs ("I lay my life upon the altar of desire — the seen, the sensed, that which appeals to me, the satisfaction of my need"). They have a need for that which gives material pleasure, feeds pride, and satisfies the questioning of the mind ("a need for that which is material, for that which feeds emotion, that satisfies the mind"). They also have a need for simple, unambiguous answers to their demands for truth and ways to serve ("that answers my demand for truth, for service").

Owing to these characteristics, they have constructed a mental concept of a sensed intuitive goal ("my vision of the goal"). Their devotion to that concept now determines the thoughts they think, the beliefs they hold, the activities that meet their needs, and the viewpoints they grasp and understand ("It is the vision which I see, the dream I dream, the truth I hold, the active form which meets my need, that which I grasp and understand"). Their mental concept may take many forms: either their belief, inner peace, satisfied desire, dream, vision of reality, limited ideal, or finite thought of God ("My truth, my peace, my satisfied desire, my dream, my vision of reality, my limited ideal, my finite thought of God"). Rather than working to express the underlying intuitive goal, they observe that all the time they are struggling, fighting, and sacrificing for their own mental concept ("for these I struggle, fight and die").

The next step for aspirants is to discover the roots of their problem by using a careful process of reasoning that evokes the wisdom of the soul. As shown by the second paragraph of the technique, they come to the following conclusions. To express the goal that they intuitively sense, they must always have "love of the truth," which means devotion to spiritual reality rather than to some concept of reality. Desire reaching out for a material object is not really different from aspiration soaring upward to a lofty mental ideal ("Desire and aspiration, reaching out for that which is material or soaring upward towards the vision of reality"). Both are seeking and will find the satisfaction of self-centered needs ("must ever find their satisfaction"). For either form of satisfaction, "men work, driving themselves and irking others." Those who are devoted to spiritual truth as they interpret it, in the form of their vision and ideal, forget that their truth is limited by their own mental conceptions ("They love the truth as they interpret it; they love the vision and the dream, forgetting that the truth is limited by mind"). Such a limited ideal must be "narrow and set, one-pointed, not inclusive." Such a limited "vision touches but the outer fringe of mystery, and veils and hides reality."

There is a similarity between the third and sixth rays. During the stage of selfish influence, persons on both of these rays are extremely susceptible to glamours and illusions. Both

types experience futility because their activities are largely inef-
fective. The third-ray person must learn to have "love of truth,"
which means devotion to clear comprehension regarding the
phenomenal world. On the other hand, the sixth-ray person
must learn to have "love of *the* truth," which means devotion to
the spiritual reality that lies behind the phenomenal world.

The symbolic statement for the sixth ray places its main
emphasis on the probationary path. By comparing the statements for the different rays, it can be seen that the sixth-ray
technique has the largest number of words dedicated to that
particular stage. There is a reason for this emphasis: It is relatively time-consuming and difficult for sixth-ray aspirants to
discover the roots of their problem because of their complete
assurance that they are devoted to and serving worthwhile religious, political, or social causes. Before they can have a true
spiritual unfoldment, it is necessary for them to continue with
self-observation and careful reasoning until they develop a
cycle of doubt, perhaps even a temporary agnosticism, and
restore a more balanced way of life. In particular, they must
discover and admit to such vices as sectarianism, prejudice,
fiery anger, self-deception, and superstition and then establish
the opposite virtues, such as tolerance, balance, serenity, common sense, and devotion to the truth. When they successfully
reorient their lives, they attain the first initiation.

During the path of discipleship, sixth-ray disciples receive
intuitively the series of lessons outlined in the final paragraph
of the technique. The first lesson is to "run not so straight." In
other words, it is necessary to achieve the arduous task of
dissociating from those ideals that are narrow, set, one-
pointed, and not inclusive. Adherence to such ideals leads to
being involved with outer forms without any awareness of
inner truth ("The path that you are on leads to the outer circle
of the life of God"). For devotees, it leads to being lost in their
devotion; for idealists, to being driven by their ideals; and for
followers, to running blindly after their masters ("the line goes
forward to the outer rim").

Second, practice receptive meditation, which involves increasing alignment ("Stand") after having raised the consciousness into the highest point of the mental body ("at the centre"). The recommended approach is as follows: Raise the consciousness as high in the head as possible; with full concentrated interest and attention, become oriented to the soul; achieve a position of *listening*, which means being consciously ready for impression; see how long this position can be held while keeping the mind alert and not relinquishing the sense of personal identity; and then note (if it comes) the emergence of some clear thought, clarification of some bewilderment, or expansion of some mental perception into an intuition.[40]

Because disciples at this stage identify with the personality, receptive meditation tends to be dualistic in nature: They try to receive guidance from a source conceived of as being beyond or higher than themselves. Unfortunately, there are several dangers with this approach. If they have a strong determination to eliminate their thoughts, then they may fixate on some thought or image and enter a hypnotic trance. The trance condition is definitely undesirable, because the personality is separated from the soul and is unable to receive guidance from the soul. In addition, they may open the emotional body to influences coming from discarnate entities, which could lead to such problems as mediumistic possession. It is important to emphasize: The goal should be to receive intuitive understanding from one's own soul rather than messages from the watching denizens of the inner planes. Because of these dangers, receptive meditation should be practiced in such a way that only the apex of the mind is open and receptive, while the lower aspects of the personality are closed to any extraneous interferences. Furthermore, to avoid the possibility of a hypnotic trance, this type of meditation should be practiced for only as long as the meditator can maintain a recollection of who he is and what he is doing.[41]

Third, "look on every side," which means overcome the partisan spirit by developing breadth of vision and a right sense of proportion. Disciples should learn to welcome all visions if they serve to lift other people, all truths if they are agents of revelation to other minds, and all ideals if they act as incentives to others. They should learn to share in them all, while receiving their own guidance and direction from the practice of receptive meditation.

Fourth, "die not for outer forms," which means cease being devoted to external conditions such as a cause, teacher, creed, person, duty, or responsibility. This type of devotion may seem to be beautiful and noble, but it is actually harmful because it can obliterate the wider vision and shut the person within a tiny circle of his own making. Because sixth-ray disciples are especially susceptible to this type of difficulty, they need to discover and then dissipate such aspects of their desire life as the glamour of devotion, the glamour of adherence to forms and persons, the glamour of loyalties and creeds, the glamour of sentimentality, and the glamour of fanaticism. While the major effort during the stage of reorientation was establishing new virtues, the effort here is discovering and then dissipating the glamours that underlie the vices.[42]

And fifth, "forget not God, Who dwells behind the vision." In the past, sixth-ray disciples were able to sense intuitive glimpses of a noble truth or goal, but they converted those glimpses into mental concepts and then became emotionally devoted to those concepts. Thus, their earlier difficulties occurred because they did not differentiate between reality and a symbol of reality, such as between God and a vision of God, or between the divine plan for humanity and a narrow ideal. But now they need to make that differentiation and be devoted only to reality.[43]

It is important to notice the order in which the lessons for each ray are given. For instance, the instruction on glamour is the first lesson given to a disciple in the second-ray technique. This position occurs because second-ray disciples have an innate faculty of clear perception that usually enables them to be fully aware of their emotional distortions. On the other hand, the instruction on glamour is the fourth lesson given in the sixth-ray technique. It is relatively hard for a sixth-ray disciple to admit being held by a glamour, particularly a glamour having a spiritual connotation. Thus, the instruction on glamour is preceded by earlier instructions on dissociating from narrow ideals, practicing receptive meditation, and developing breadth of vision.[44]

When there has been success in following these instructions, the disciple attains the second initiation and becomes ready to practice the method of occult meditation appropriate for the sixth ray. The final sentence of the technique describes this meditation with the words "love more your fellow men." The approach is to become polarized in the soul and then express devotion through the soul. While devotion expressing itself through the personality engenders fanaticism and is frequently cruel, devotion expressing itself through the soul is love and inclusiveness plus understanding. This sixth-ray meditation could be called "the method of divine fanaticism" because the disciple is willing to bend every faculty, make every effort, and sacrifice even the personality in order to serve the divine plan.[45]

The Sanskrit word *bhakti* means devotion, and it refers to the devotion of the personality. The Sanskrit word *para-bhakti* means supreme devotion, and it refers to the devotion of the soul. In bhakti yoga, the path of devotion, the effort is to move from expressing bhakti to expressing para-bhakti. Swami Vivekananda describes the goal of bhakti yoga as follows:

> Love of the pleasures of the senses and of the intellect is all made dim and thrown aside and cast into the shade by the love of God Himself. That love of God grows and assumes a form called para-bhakti, or supreme devotion. Forms vanish, rituals fly away, books are superseded; images, temples, churches, religions and sects, countries and nationalities — all

these little limitations and bondages fall away naturally from him who knows this love of God.[46]

As shown by this quotation, bhakti yoga has a perspective and
goal similar to that of the sixth-ray technique.

The Self-Realization Fellowship founded by Paramahansa
Yogananda is an example of a religious activity that embodies
many of the ideas of the sixth-ray technique. In addition to
encouraging meditation and devotion to God, this organization emphasizes the importance of recognizing the basic unity
that exists among all religions. One of their properties is a lake
shrine that incorporates the symbols from all major religious
traditions.[47]

Ray Seven

"I seek to bring the two together. The plan is in my
hands. How shall I work? Where lay the emphasis?
In the far distance stands the One Who *Is*. Here at
my hand is form, activity, substance, and desire. Can
I relate these and fashion thus a form for God? Where
shall I send my thought, my power the word that I
can speak?

"I, at the centre, stand, the worker in the field of
magic. I know some rules, some magical controls,
some Words of Power, some forces which I can direct.
What shall I do? Danger there is. The task that I have
undertaken is not easy of accomplishment, yet I love
power. I love to see the forms emerge, created by my
mind, and do their work, fulfill the plan and disappear. I can create. The rituals of the Temple of the
Lord are known to me. How shall I work?

"*Love not the work.* Let love of God's eternal Plan
control your life, your mind, your hand, your eye.
Work towards the unity of plan and purpose which

must find its lasting place on earth. Work with the
Plan; focus upon your share in that great work."

The word goes forth from soul to form: "Stand in the
centre of the pentagram, drawn upon that high place
in the East within the light which ever shines. From
that illumined centre work. Leave not the pentagram. Stand steady in the midst. Then draw a line
from that which is without to that which is within and
see the Plan take form."[48]

The seventh is called the ray of ceremonial order or
magic. Seventh-ray individuals are workers in magic in the
sense that they know how to translate their mental images into
physical reality. To be successful, magical work requires knowledge of appropriate *rules*, *controls*, and *words of power*. Perhaps
the best way to understand these concepts is through a series of
examples. First, consider a businessman who organizes
employees and machinery to produce material goods. He is a
magical worker in the following sense: he begins with a mental
picture of the way his factory should look and then uses his
organizing power to manifest that picture in the form of a
productive factory. However, to manifest his picture, it is necessary for him to know certain rules, including the legal, finan-
cial, and material rules for operating a business; know certain
controls, namely, methods of controlling employees, such as
through a pleasant environment and adequate compensation;
and know certain words of power, such as effective ways of
speaking that convey clarity and motivation to employees.

As a second example, consider a sculptor. She is also a
magical worker because she is able to produce material forms
and patterns that reflect her mental vision of beauty. She also
needs to know certain rules, controls, and words of power. In
this case, she needs to know the physical rules and properties of
the medium with which she is working; how to control her
mind, hands, and medium while sculpting; and effective ways

of speaking to herself for the purpose of being motivated to complete her task.

As a third example, consider a practitioner of one of the "new thought" or metaphysical religions, such as Science of Mind.[49] Metaphysics teaches that physical conditions are reflections of the subconscious mind, which in turn can be affected by the conscious mind. By changing thinking patterns, metaphysical practitioners try to improve various aspects of the material world such as their health, prosperity, and relationships. To be successful, they need to know the rules governing the interaction between the conscious mind, subconscious mind, and physical experience; how to control the conscious mind so that it remains focussed on a chosen theme; and appropriate affirmations that, when spoken, can affect the subconscious mind in the desired way.

The first paragraph of Bailey's symbolic technique describes how individuals undergo the crisis of evocation for the seventh ray. Due to the basic quality of the soul, which is magic, they intuitively sense that there must be a divine plan and that their purpose is to help manifest that plan in the material world ("I seek to bring the two together"). Because of this purpose, they have found some written plans for a better world, perhaps in the area of politics, religion, or economics ("The plan is in my hands"). However, they are confused about how they should work and where they should lay their emphasis ("How shall I work? Where lay the emphasis?"). This confusion is present because they have not been guided by the spiritual dimension of life, which they think of as being in the far distance away ("In the far distance stands the One Who Is"). At this point in their evolution, they know how to carry out the process of magic within the context of their chosen profession: how dense physical form can be affected by etheric or vital activity, and how the latter can be directed by mental substance when the proper emotional desire is present ("Here at my hand is form, activity, substance, and desire"). They ask themselves: Can these different types of forces be related to build a physical form that would embody the spirit of God ("Can I relate these and fashion thus a form for God")? To answer this question, they ask themselves a more basic one: What physical form should appear as a manifestation of their thoughts, through the application of their words of power ("Where shall I send my thought, my power the word that I can speak")? Being confused about the answers to these questions, they call on the understanding of the soul for guidance.

The first step that aspirants are guided to take on the path of probation is self-observation, and the second paragraph describes this step. By becoming focused at the center of self-observation ("I, at the centre"), they increase their alignment ("stand") and then examine their activities "in the field of magic." They acknowledge knowing "some rules, some magical controls, some Words of Power" that enable them to direct certain forces. Being confused about what should be done with those forces ("What shall I do?"), they decide to observe their underlying motives. Because magical work can stimulate their lower nature, they see there is danger of swinging into a maelstrom of work in which they are materially minded, selfishly ambitious, and unloving ("Danger there is").

The last portion of the second paragraph describes the next step on the path of probation. Through a careful process of reasoning, seventh-ray aspirants come to the following conclusions. The task they have undertaken, which is working to improve physical conditions, is impeded by a number of vices in their character ("The task that I have undertaken is not easy of accomplishment"). For instance, these vices include bigotry, narrowness, superficial judgments, over-indulgence in self-opinions, and especially pride ("yet I love power"). Consequently, they need to prepare by applying the process of magic to themselves. Since magic involves translating mental pictures into physical reality, their approach begins by visualizing a detailed mental picture of how they want to work with the divine plan ("I love to see the forms emerge, created by my mind, and do their work, fulfill the plan and disappear"). In this way, they can create a mental image of themselves as expressing the virtues that are opposite to their vices ("I can create"). These virtues include tolerance, wide-mindedness, gentleness, humility, and love. They also know the rituals needed to translate the mental image of the ideal self into physical reality, thereby transforming themselves into dedicated physical instruments of God ("The rituals of the Temple of the Lord are known to me"). These rituals include using various types of meditation exercises at regular times of the day, and chapter 3 describes several exercises that might be used. Their final conclusion is that they must invoke the illumination of the soul for guidance during this work ("How shall I work?").

When there has been success in this process of reorientation, the first initiation is attained. Because of their desire to build a better world, seventh-ray disciples receive intuitively the series of instructions listed in the third paragraph. The first instruction is "love not the work." In other words, they need to make a conscious effort to discover and then dissipate the various types of pride that could arise when working with the powers of the soul. These emotional distortions lie behind their vices and may include the glamour of magical work, the glamour of that which brings together, the glamour of the mysterious and the secret, and the glamour of the emerging manifested forces. Chapter 3 describes a method for dissipating glamours that combines raja yoga with the process of magic.

Second, "let love of God's eternal Plan control your life, your mind, your hand, your eye." Note this sequence. By avoiding glamour and letting devotion for the divine plan control the desire life, the mind becomes poised and peaceful. The mind can then receive the divine plan from the soul, which is received in the form of an intuitive understanding of the world need and how to meet that need. The desire life and inner thoughts determine both physical activity and how the world is perceived. When the emotions and mind are dedicated to the divine plan, the hands can be used to help manifest that plan, and the next immediate step can be taken as it becomes apparent before the eyes.

Third, "work towards the unity of plan and purpose which must find its lasting place on earth." Because God in His wisdom has chosen to limit Himself, the work of evolution proceeds solely through the medium of His chosen builders and under the direction of those individuals whose lives are being transformed through soul contact and creative service. In particular, three different groups of workers are responsible for implementing the divine plan. The highest group consists of initiates of the fourth or higher initiation. After registering the divine purpose, they formulate the divine plan on the level of intuitive ideas. The middle group consists of disciples and initiates of the first three initiations. After receiving the intuitive ideas during the silence of their meditations, they transform those ideas into acceptable mental ideals. The lowest group consists of intelligent aspirants. They respond to the mental ideals, generally in the form of written documents, and then help to manifest those ideals on earth. The workers in each group should cooperate with the other members of their group, as well as with the other groups.[50]

And fourth, "work with the Plan; focus upon your share in that great work." Because disciples are part of the middle group, their task is to work with the divine plan as they intuitively receive it during their meditations. To achieve that end, they need to do the following: deepen their experience of meditation, so that there is a more frequent illumining of the mind by the light of the soul; learn to distinguish between the divine plan and any ambition they might have for their own lives or for their chosen fields of service; and learn to recognize the part they may play in the evolutionary process, while having the humility and sense of proportion to be a tiny part of a greater whole. When the divine plan is truly intuited at first hand, then constructive efforts are inevitable. But when this plan is only partially realized or ignorantly interpreted at second or third hand, there may be wasted efforts and foolish impulses.[51]

To understand the symbolism in the final paragraph of the technique, it is necessary to review some information regarding esoteric anatomy. As discussed in chapter 1, the physical body is controlled and vitalized by seven principal etheric chakras. These etheric energy centers have counterparts in the emotional body and in the mental body. According to Bailey, the mental body is controlled and vitalized by exactly five mental chakras: the mental unit, mental solar plexus, mental spleen, mental generative organs, and mental base of spine.[52] For the purposes of this commentary, it is not necessary to know the functions of these mental chakras. However, this information does enable the mental body to be symbolized with a pentagram, or five-pointed star, with each point representing one of the five mental energy centers.

When disciples have succeeded in accomplishing the earlier instructions, they attain the second initiation and become ready to practice the method of occult meditation that is appropriate for the seventh ray. Occult meditation for any ray involves carrying out the five stages of raja yoga discussed in the commentary for the fifth ray. The first three stages are concentration, meditation, and contemplation, and these stages lead to being polarized temporarily in the soul. The last two stages, illumination and inspiration, transform the intuitive knowing of the soul into a life of service on the physical plane. How these latter stages are carried out depends on the soul's ray; the method for the seventh ray is described below.

In the last paragraph of the technique, the first phrase is "the word goes forth from soul to form," which also appears in the technique for each previous ray. Except for the seventh ray, this phrase appears at the beginning of the path of discipleship, and it is meant to describe the transfer of intuitive guidance from the soul to the personality. However, for the seventh ray, this phrase appears after the second initiation, and it is meant to describe the process of white magic: manifesting an intuitive idea from the soul in physical form.

White magic necessarily has five different steps: first, receiving the intuitive idea in the mind; second, constructing a concrete mental picture of that idea; third, adding emotional desire; fourth, adding etheric vitality or activity; and fifth, adding dense physical matter. In terms of the stages of raja yoga, the first step of white magic corresponds to contemplation; the second step, to illumination; and the last three steps, to inspiration. The remaining portion of the last paragraph consists of five sentences, and each of these sentences provides concise instruction for the corresponding step in the process of white magic.

In the first step, the individual's consciousness slips out of what is called the personality and becomes polarized in the soul. The soul on its own plane becomes active, thinks in unison with all souls, taps the resources of the spiritual mind, and formulates its purposes in line with the divine plan. Meanwhile the personality is aligned ("Stand"), focused within the mental body ("in the centre of the pentagram") on the mental plane ("drawn upon that high place"), and oriented ("in the East") toward receiving intuitive ideas from the soul ("within the light which ever shines").[53]

Second, after the individual's consciousness slips back into the personality, the waiting mind becomes active and works as the interpreter and instrument of the soul ("From that illumined centre work"). The mind's effort is to convert the intuitive ideas of the soul into concrete thoughts or pictures, something that can be definitely visualized, which will later be manifested in the physical world. This process is called *white magic* because the individual is guided by the illumination of the soul. In contrast, *black magic* refers to using magical abilities for the purpose of fulfilling self-centered ambition. White and black magicians may use similar methods when manifesting their respective forms on the physical plane. The essential difference between the two is in how they select the forms they endeavor to build.[54]

The third step is a period of gestation in which there arises the desire to bring the vision of the soul down to earth. However, there is a danger in this work. By being relating agents between the spiritual and physical dimensions of life, disciples attract an inflow of power that comes from both directions: inspired ideas from the spiritual dimension and publicity, recognition, and adulation from the physical dimension. If they allow themselves to be corrupted by the power of this position, then they will fall into the practice of black magic. To avoid this danger and possibility, they must continually observe their emotional reactions and maintain the proper motives, which requires that they not leave the condition of being focused in the mental body ("Leave not the pentagram").

The fourth step involves using knowledge of appropriate rules, controls, and words of power to direct activities on the physical plane. While in the midst of these building processes, disciples must steadily maintain their alignment ("Stand steady in the midst") to do three things at the same time: preserve the mental picture; maintain the proper emotional feeling; and direct the physical activities.

The clue to understanding the entire process of white magic is this: potencies produce precipitation. For the fifth and final step in the process, this clue can be expressed as follows: a dense physical form is an outer effect, or precipitation, of inner causes. When the proper thought, feeling, and activity are present and when sense data from the physical plane ("Then draw a line from that which is without") are registered as perceptions in the mind ("to that which is within"), the divine plan will be seen as taking dense physical form ("and see the Plan take form").[55]

The Technique of Integration for the seventh ray employs the terminology of ceremonial magic, the ancient art of invoking and controlling spirits. It was once thought that a magician could control the invisible inhabitants of the spirit world through ritualistic ceremonies that applied the power invested in certain words and symbols. The pentagram, or five-pointed star, was one of the symbols most often used. In medieval alchemy, this symbol was known as "the sign of the cloven hoof" and also as "the star of Bethlehem." In Gnostic schools, this symbol was called "the blazing star." The pentagram was sometimes considered as representing the human body, with the five points symbolizing the head, two arms, and two legs. When the pentagram was upright, with a single point representing the head directed upward, this symbol represented wisdom, order, initiation, and victory. But when the pentagram was reversed, with one point directed downward, this symbol represented evil, confusion, profanation, and death.[56]

As a brief summary for this chapter, the distinctive aspect of each Technique of Integration is expressed with a single word: for ray one, inclusion; for ray two, centralization; for ray three, stillness; for ray four, steadfastness; for ray five, detachment; for ray six, dissociation; and for ray seven, illumination.[57]

Chapter 3

Applications

The information on the seven rays given in the preceding chapters is worthwhile only if it can be applied in daily life and tested in the crucible of firsthand experience. Because the typology of the seven rays provides a classification of the basic quality of the soul, this typology can help explain and clarify the experiences of someone who has begun the process of integrating personality with soul. A number of other typologies have been devised in psychology that are useful in other contexts. This chapter demonstrates the practicality of the information on the seven rays by considering the following topics: psychotherapy, ray analysis, subjective guidance, self-observation, character building, emotional purification, and service.

Psychotherapy

Human evolution proceeds by a series of integrations. An average adult has already achieved the following integrations: between the dense physical body and the etheric or vital body;

between these two and the emotional or sentient body; and between these three and the lower concrete mind. The next step is integrating these four aspects so that they function as a whole, producing a coordinated personality. An advanced adult is working on integrating personality with soul. This section discusses how a therapist might facilitate each of these integrations. There are also higher integrations, but these are the only ones considered here.

Each of the foregoing processes of integration begins when the individual experiences a sense of cleavage or lack of wholeness, and it ends when a new coordination or synthesis is achieved. Because of possible frustration and intense suffering, one may need the understanding help of a trained psychotherapist before the new synthesis can occur. The following basic premises should govern the activity of a therapist when dealing with these situations. Any psychological difficulty is universal and not unique to the patient. The sense of uniqueness should be negated in the patient because such a sense could lead to feelings of separation from others and becoming engrossed in one's own difficulty. The crisis being faced by the patient indicates progress and opportunity, rather than disaster and failure. The patient should be helped to realize that each human being, and the human race as a whole, progresses through similar crises. The power to produce the needed integration and to end the cycle of sensed duality lies within the patient. The patient's discomfort, lack of coordination, and pain are symptoms of aspiration, and these symptoms are reactions of the lower integrated aspects to the higher aspect that is next to be integrated. The coming higher aspect is relatively more powerful than the lower waiting ones because it is positive and dynamic, while the others are negative and receptive. The patient's imaginative capacity to act "as if" holds the solution to the problem. The bridge between the lower aspects and the higher can be constructed by using the creative imagination.[1]

Suggestions are given separately for assisting the integration of each type of cleavage. First consider etheric cleavage, referring to a gap between the dense physical and etheric bodies. An infant generally is able to complete the integration of this type of cleavage. Parents can aid this process through proper prenatal care, nutritious and balanced diet, and developing in infants a positive sense of themselves. When etheric cleavage occurs in an adult, the result is a psychotic mental illness. In such an illness, the patient essentially has become stuck in a hypnotic trance, implying that there is no self-consciousness, no power of centralized control, and no capacity to make plans. For instance the patient could be suffering from idiocy, deep depression, obsession, possession, multiple personality, or schizophrenia. The less serious forms of this type of problem often can be cured by purely material means that increase the patient's vitality, such as building up the etheric body through sunshine, vitamins, balanced diet, and proper exercise, plus correct treatment and balancing of the endocrine gland system.[2]

A child generally is able to complete the integration of the cleavage between the etheric and emotional bodies. Parents and teachers can aid this process by developing the sense of fantasy in children and by training them to make choices. These two factors are the evidence of the child's innate divinity. The sense of fantasy brings into play the creative imagination and perception of beauty. Making choices helps to unfold the use of directed purpose and includes such considerations as why, wherefore, and to what end. Cleavage between the etheric and emotional bodies can also occur in adults, producing some of the problem cases found in mental institutions. A therapist can bring about the self-releasing of many of these problem cases by assisting patients in developing their sense of fantasy and training them to make choices.[3]

Adolescents are generally working on bridging the cleavage between their emotional and mental bodies. This cleavage becomes apparent when there is awareness of having dominant and compelling desires, plus the awareness of being unable to satisfy those desires. Because of this cleavage, they may feel frustrated and depressed, become inactive, escape through various fantasies, and even consider suicide. Or they may be compulsively driven to achieve success and fulfill desires. However, the best approach is to begin using one's mind to discriminate between essentials and nonessentials and between right direction and wrong goals. A therapist can aid this process by helping patients to recognize, understand, and use their assets, eliminate impossible goals and the associated frustrations, and recognize the goals that can be potentially achieved.[4]

The average adult experiences a lack of coordination among the dense physical, etheric, emotional, and mental bodies, which can be thought of as being cleavage between the elements of personality and the personality considered as a whole. This cleavage leads to lack of ability to concentrate, breaks in the continuity of interests, unfinished tasks, and frustration. At this stage, people generally realize that they must make some living contribution to their environment to evoke a desirable response in return. Furthermore, to make this contribution, they generally realize that they must do two things: coordinate the separate parts of the personality into one whole plus study and use their surroundings — the whole of which the personality is a part — in such a way that the cleavage between themselves and their environment is ended. Although their motives are entirely selfish and materialistic, they learn to coordinate their personality to make a contribution to others.

Those having difficulty in achieving this coordination can be aided during therapy in several ways: by being encouraged to have proper exercise, diet, and training for the physical body, which is helpful because physical coordination is an outer expression of personality coordination; assisted in eliminating the sense of sin or guilt, including such concomitants as revolt, suspicion, and an inferiority complex; aided in interpreting and appreciating the achievements in their lives; and helped in developing the power to recognize and meet the needs in their surrounding community, leading to a sense of pride in themselves. For instance, there should be right interests, education, and vocational training; a search for and development of any creative ability, such as in art, literature, or music, that would fulfill the desire to be noticed and to contribute; and a formulation of an inner program, intelligently compiled, that would develop and express abilities while avoiding activities doomed to failure.[5]

It can be seen from this discussion that a person evolves in consciousness by recognizing that a particular cleavage exists, bridging that cleavage through struggle and effort, and then repeating that same cycle on a higher level through the recognition of a new cleavage. For those who have successfully coordinated their personality, the next cycle begins when they recognize that cleavage exists between personality and soul. This occurs when they sense the basic quality of the soul's ray and contrast that quality with the activities of daily life. The recognition of this cleavage leads to what is called the "crisis of evocation," because they begin to seek the guidance of the soul.

When a patient is going through the crisis of evocation, the therapist should treat the difficulty as a sign of progress, showing a relatively high point on the evolutionary scale. This condition should be regarded as warranting explanation and understanding but no real concern. However, if the therapist treats the difficulty as a disease of the patient's mind and attempts to bring relief by eliminating the symptoms, the work of the patient's soul may be delayed.[6]

For the final case considered here, suppose that the patient has undergone the crisis of evocation and has begun the process of integrating personality with soul. Because the patient is being intuitively guided from within to apply the Technique of Integration for the appropriate ray, the best approach to therapy is assisting in that process, which helps the patient in *consciously* bringing in the power of the soul. Because the patient is now fairly evolved, the soul can impress the personality via the mind. When the power of the soul pours through the personality life, all aspects of the lower nature become cleansed and purified. The initial step in this type of therapy is identifying the patient's ray, and the next section discusses how this identification can be made.[7] The therapist-patient relationship is now similar to the guru-student relationship in yoga. As described by Paramahansa Yogananda, the wise guru guides students onto the paths of the different yogas (karma, jnana, raja, or bhakti), according to each student's natural tendencies.[8]

Ray Analysis

A *ray* is defined as a particular quality of energy, which implies that a given ray can be expressed by different energies having various form aspects. Because individuals consist of multiple energies, they are affected by multiple rays: the rays of the physical body, emotional body, mental body, coordinated personality, and soul. Although the emphasis in this book has been on the soul, each of these other constituent energies also expresses a particular ray quality.

Early in life, everyone is governed primarily by the ray of the physical body. Later we are governed by the ray of the emotional body and then by the ray of the mental body. During these stages, it is not possible to say definitely what the ray of the soul is because only the rays of these other energies are apparent.

During the stage of selfish influence, the individual has attained a degree of alignment with the soul and utilizes some of the powers of the soul, albeit in a distorted way, to coordinate the personality and achieve the separative ambitions of the personality. Consequently, during this stage, both the personality ray and the soul ray begin to be apparent. According to Bailey, the soul ray consists of seven different subrays, which can be thought of as being seven different vibrations or notes, and the personality ray is one of those subrays.[9]

The relationship between the personality ray and the soul ray can be thought of in the following way. Everyone is born into the physical world with certain limitations of circumstance. These limitations are called karma in Eastern philosophy and the ring-pass-not in esoteric philosophy. Because of these limitations, each person is able to accomplish only certain purposes, rather than all possible purposes. For instance, one may be forced by circumstances into activities that are intrinsically difficult, while occupations for which one may have a natural talent are closed. The seven subrays of the soul ray represent the full spectrum of soul powers that are potentially available to an individual. The personality ray is that particular subray that is primarily developed and expressed in response to one's circumstances.[10]

In her books, Bailey classifies the personality ray with the same typology that is used for the soul ray. Thus, the personality ray for an individual is either the first ray of will, second ray of love-wisdom, third ray of active intelligence, fourth ray of harmony through conflict, fifth ray of concrete knowledge, sixth ray of devotion, or seventh ray of ceremonial order. The personality ray indicates the individual's outer occupation or career, appearance, life trend, goal, and purpose. On the other hand, the soul ray indicates one's basic quality and method of accomplishment.[11]

For instance, suppose that an individual's personality ray is the fifth ray of concrete knowledge, while the soul ray is the second ray of love-wisdom. By definition, the personality ray is a subray of the soul ray. Thus, the personality ray is actually the fifth subray of the second ray of love-wisdom. What does this relationship really mean? Having a second-ray soul, the individual's basic approach is one of expansion and inclusion. With a fifth-ray personality, the individual's primary activity in life is to apply that approach for the goal of apprehending knowledge. Thus, intellectual expansion is achieved by using a second-ray method with a fifth-ray application.[12]

Table 1. Examples of the Seven Ray Types, According to Various Sources

Ray	Assagioli	Bailey	Creme	Eastcott	Hodson
One	Alexander the Great Julius Caesar Julius Evola Napoleon I F. Nietzsche Max Stirner Richard Wagner	Kemal Ataturk Otto Bismarck H. P. Blavatsky Julius Caesar H. H. Kitchener Abraham Lincoln Napoleon I F. D. Roosevelt	Alexander the Great Abraham Lincoln D. MacArthur Richard Wagner	Alexander the Great W. Churchill Adolf Hitler Genghis Khan B. Mussolini Napoleon I F. D. Roosevelt	W. Churchill King George V D. MacArthur G. S. Patton
Two	Buddha	Buddha Patanjali Plato Sankaracharya	Buddha R. W. Emerson D. Erasmus Carl G. Jung	Buddha Pope John Paul II Mother Teresa of Calcutta	Buddha
Three	Auguste Compte Confucius Henry Ford Hyppolyte Taine		Auguste Compte Confucius Isaac Newton Adam Smith	Henry Ford	B. L. Montgomery J. C. Smuts
Four	Leonardo da Vinci M. Maeterlinck G. A. Rossini W. Shakespeare	Leonardo da Vinci W. Shakespeare	L. Beethoven Leonardo da Vinci Maurice Ravel Auguste Renoir	Claude Debussy F. Delius Leonardo da Vinci M. Maeterlinck Maurice Ravel W. Shakespeare	John Keats W. Shakespeare

Table 1. Continued

Ray	Assagioli	Bailey	Creme	Eastcott	Hodson
Five	René Descartes Immanuel Kant	Thomas Edison	Archimedes V. I. Lenin Louis Pasteur Thucydides	René Descartes Albert Einstein Immanuel Kant	Sherlock Holmes
Six	St. Paul Don Quixote	Jesus Alfred Tennyson Woodrow Wilson	Jesus St. Luke Martin Luther Alfred Tennyson	Jesus Mohammed St. Paul	St. Clare St. Francis Bro. Lawrence
Seven		Marie Curie Pierre Curie Robert Millikan	Aristotle Francis Bacon Roger Bacon Annie Besant	Marie Curie Pierre Curie	

Sources: R. Assagioli, *Psychosynthesis Typology*, 22 – 23, 35, 43 – 44, 55 – 56, 58, 63, 73; A. A. Bailey, *The Destiny of the Nations*, 16; A. A. Bailey, *Discipleship in the New Age*, vol. 1, xii; A. A. Bailey, *Esoteric Astrology*, 564; A. A. Bailey, *Esoteric Psychology*, vol. 1, 202, 209, 226; A. A. Bailey, *Esoteric Psychology*, vol. 2, 292; A. A. Bailey, *The Externalisation of the Hierarchy*, 278, 297 – 298, 578, 685; A. A. Bailey, *Telepathy and the Etheric Vehicle*, 5; A. A. Bailey, *A Treatise on Cosmic Fire*, 456; B. Creme, *Maitreya's Mission*, 385 – 402; M. J. Eastcott, *The Seven Rays of Energy*, 23, 30, 44, 46, 50, 61, 69, 73, 77, 81; G. Hodson, *The Seven Human Temperaments*, 14 – 18, 23, 29 – 32, 37, 42, 43.

Another example might be helpful. A first-ray personality may indicate the career of a soldier. As discussed in the introductory remarks to each ray in chapter 1, an individual with any soul ray can be a soldier, but the approach to that career depends on the soul ray. For instance, a first-ray soul would indicate leadership ability; a second-ray soul, wise planning during battle; a third-ray soul, an intellectual approach to military tactics; a fourth-ray soul, possible recklessness during combat; a fifth-ray soul, an interest in artillery and engineering; a sixth-ray soul, a ferocious fighter; and a seventh-ray soul, a good supply officer.

In either chapter 1 or 2, the symbolic statement given under the heading for each ray is applicable to someone having that particular soul ray while having any one of the seven types of personality rays. How can the soul ray for someone be discerned? The soul ray can be identified only after the individual has achieved some alignment with the soul and is utilizing some of the soul's powers. If such alignment and utilization are present, then the following could be done.

First, consider the individual's career. Because the soul is an indicator of quality, not appearance, it is necessary to look at the approach taken to the career rather than at the career itself. However, if the person has shifted careers late in life, then that shift might indicate the soul ray. For instance, if a person was formerly a creative artist but suddenly takes a deep and profound interest in mathematics, then it might be inferred that the influence of a second-ray soul is becoming predominant.[13]

Second, examine the individual's hobbies, particularly those that were begun after some alignment with the soul had been achieved. Generally speaking, our vocations indicate our personality ray, and our avocations indicate our soul ray. For instance, if one pursues scientific investigation as a hobby, one might be responding to a fifth-ray soul.

Third, examine the organizations with which the individual is affiliated. As discussed in chapter 2, there is an organized system of thought that represents the Technique of Integration for each ray. If given the opportunity, people would seek to be affiliated with an organization that embodied their particular technique because such an affiliation would provide an outer confirmation for the intuitive instruction they are receiving from within. However, they may not be able to find an organization that embodies their particular path in a pure form. For example, the only opportunity may be to join a Christian church. But which denomination do they choose? And within that denomination, which teachings do they emphasize and which ones do they ignore?

And fourth, examine the individual's personality. What is the nature of the inner conflict that led to the crisis of evocation? What strengths and weaknesses are evident? As discussed in chapter 2, each ray is associated with characteristic virtues, vices, and glamours.

Proceeding through these four steps, you are encouraged to attempt a ray analysis for both yourself and those you know. If there is truth concerning the typology of the seven rays, then a basic consistency will be discovered in the foregoing areas. As an example, Table 1 on pages 94–95 gives the soul ray for a number of well-known individuals according to several sources. At the beginning, the reader should regard the information about the seven rays as being only a hypothesis. However, Bailey predicts that, by studying oneself and others with care, this hypothesis eventually will change into a living fact.[14]

Subjective Guidance

As discussed in chapters 1 and 2, the crisis of evocation marks the beginning of the spiritual path. During this crisis, aspirants realize that they must change their method, direction, and attitude, and so they begin to call on the wisdom of the soul for guidance. While a number of spiritual groups acknowledge that there is such a thing as subjective guidance, much confusion exists regarding this topic for the following reason: There is often a failure to differentiate between the various sources of subjective information that can be contacted.

It may be helpful to review some contemporary teachings regarding subjective guidance. A number of groups instruct their members to meditate in the following way: Use a process of autosuggestion to enter a state of trance, and then notice the various urges, voices, inclinations, commands, or revelations that may be present. Depending on the school of thought, this guidance is said to come from the guru, God, spirit guide, higher self, or voice of the Christ within. However, a person in a hypnotic trance is not a channel for the soul, lacks control over the process, and is unable to check the source of any received information. Through this activity, one could become a trance medium. Such a medium may be receiving accurate information from the subjective realm but has forfeited free will and is little better than an instinctual animal or an empty shell that an obsessing entity can occupy and use.[15]

Heads of esoteric or spiritualistic organizations often claim to be in direct communication with a "Master of the Wisdom," or perhaps with the entire "Hierarchy of Masters," and expect their members to give prompt unquestioning obedience to the orders that are said to be passed down from the Masters. The goal of a similar relationship is held out as an inducement to the members; aspirants are led to believe that someday they will hear their own spirit teacher's voice, giving them guidance and telling them what to do. However, the goal of a true esoteric teaching is to put one consciously in touch with one's own soul and not with some discarnate entity.[16]

Some religious groups teach that the will of God can take the form of difficult life circumstances from which there is no possible escape. With this teaching, a person learns to bear difficulty by calling it destiny or karma or an expression of God's will. Rather than viewing the problem as a lesson to be mastered and overcome, one develops a spirit of submission and acquiescence. When a person deeply accepts this teaching, it becomes part of the subconscious mind. One may then hear an inner voice calling for submission and may regard it as God's voice, while failing to recognize that this voice is one's own. However, life does not demand submission and acquiescence; it demands effort, the separation of high values from the undesirable, and a cultivation of a spirit of fight that will eventually lead to useful spiritual activity.[17]

There are also many groups of people who practice various types of yoga and meditation. Although some of these groups are working with real knowledge and therefore safely, others are profoundly ignorant about both techniques and the results that can be expected from their efforts. Because the latter groups generally use methods that shut out the physical plane, a major result is to orient the person to an inner subjective world. The mind nature is seldom evoked, and the processes that are pursued often leave the mind unawakened and the brain quiescent. Because both the physical and mental planes are shut out, these people often contact only the emotional or astral plane but not the truly spiritual plane of souls.[18]

Ignorant neophytes may create much difficulty for themselves if they seek to be guided subjectively in a blind and unreasoning way. They may eventually forfeit their most divine possession, free will, and become just an impressionable automaton. Suppose they do receive some subjective information regarding their problems or life situation. What are some of the possible sources for that information?

Neophytes looking to a particular person on the physical plane for help, such as a guru or therapist, may know fairly well what the instructor would say in a given circumstance. As a result, their inner information may simply be coming from their own associative memory. Because this information may seem to be coming from an extraneous source, they may interpret it as coming from the voice of God. Or if they have a powerful coordinated personality, then the ambitions and desires of that personality may become impressed on their consciousness but in such a way that they interpret those impressions as coming from an extraneous source. Or if their practices and techniques produce an introverted attitude, then the wishes, aspirations, and tendencies of the subconscious mind may rise to the surface of consciousness, which they may then interpret as being from the voice of God.[19]

However, the guidance may in fact be coming from an extraneous source. The neophyte may have tuned in telepathically on the minds of others on the physical plane, and the resulting guidance can be good, bad, or indifferent in quality. Or methods may have been used that developed a psychic ability, where the latter is defined as the capacity to receive information from the astral plane. The two most common psychic abilities are clairaudience and clairvoyance. People experience clairaudience by having thoughts that they did not consciously originate; they experience clairvoyance by seeing images that they did not deliberately form. The astral plane is full of thoughtforms that can be contacted through psychic abilities and then be interpreted as conveying guidance. Because these thoughtforms can masquerade as famous beings, such as Jesus or Buddha, the neophyte may be completely deceived by them. Discarnate entities can also be contacted through psychic abilities, and these entities can range in character from the very good to the very bad. Because there are undesirable forces and entities, it is a mistake to give blind and unquestioning acceptance to any form of guidance.[20]

Of course, guidance can also come from the individual's own soul when contact has been made through proper meditation, discipline, and service. Because the soul is the vehicle for abstract thought and contemplation, this type of subjective guidance is experienced as an inner understanding, rather than as information received from an extraneous source. It is important to emphasize that guidance from the soul is not based on psychic ability and has nothing to do with trance conditions, mediumship, clairaudience, or clairvoyance. Individuals evoke the understanding of the soul through a process of alignment in which they slowly transfer their polarization into the soul.

By reviewing the symbolic statements given in chapter 2, it can be seen that the word *stand*, which symbolizes alignment, appears at least once within each Technique of Integration. Furthermore, this word appears at least once for each stage of the spiritual path: crisis of evocation, path of probation, first initiation, and second initiation. This usage indicates that the process of alignment is gradual and progressive: at each stage of the path, the individual makes an effort to increase alignment in a way that is appropriate for that particular stage.

As discussed in chapter 1, an individual has three focal points of perception on the mental plane: the mental body, which is the vehicle for concrete knowledge; the soul, which is the vehicle for wisdom; and the spiritual mind, which is the vehicle for insights. The process of establishing alignment occurs in three main stages: between the physical brain and the mental body; between the mental body and the soul; and between the soul and the spiritual mind. These stages correspond to the stages of concentration, meditation, and contemplation in the raja yoga technique discussed in chapter 2. When the final stage of alignment is achieved, the individual can be guided by an inner understanding that is a triple blending of the lights of knowledge, wisdom, and insight.

After the ability to receive guidance from one's own soul has been established, fostered, and stabilized, other types of spiritual guidance then become possible. For instance, the term *inspiration* refers to a transmission of understanding from a source in the subjective realm to someone on the physical plane. This transmission occurs from soul to soul, which means that it occurs on the plane of souls, referring to the higher subplanes of the mental plane. Inspiration is experienced via the crown chakra and does not utilize a psychic ability. During this process, the recipient gains an abstract or nonverbal understanding of some idea; the mind and brain may then be employed for expressing that idea in one's own thoughts and images. In contrast, mediumship refers to a transmission that is confined entirely to astral levels, is experienced via the solar plexus chakra, and utilizes a psychic ability. A trance medium receives information in the form of thoughts and images but without any understanding of that information.[21]

Self-Observation

Following the crisis of evocation, the first step in the Technique of Integration for each ray is detached self-observation, which means observing the activities of the personality from the vantage point of the soul. The approach is to cultivate constantly the observant attitude toward oneself—toward what one does, says, and thinks. By carrying the observant attitude around at all times, especially while interacting with one's associates, it is possible to discover one's underlying motives. Accomplishing this task is an arduous undertaking, and the following suggestions may be found to be helpful.

First, start each morning by deliberately applying a dis-identification exercise to three fields of observation: sensations, feelings, and thoughts. The approach is to discriminate actively between the inner self, or pure consciousness, and the fields that are the contents of consciousness. The first field is that of physical sensations produced by bodily conditions, such as comfort, fatigue, hunger, and warmth. Through calm observation, two reasons can be discovered for dis-identifying with the physical body: physical sensations are transitory and fleeting, while the inner self has stability and permanence; and those sensations can be observed, while the inner self is the observer. Because of age-long identification with the physical body, it is helpful to affirm with conviction the following fact: "I have a body, but I am not my body." This dis-identification exercise is similar to pealing the layers off an onion. After considering physical sensations, the next field of observation is that of feelings, such as desire, hope, fear, and irritation. By recognizing that feelings are countless, contradictory, and changing, and that they can be observed, understood, and then dominated, it is possible to realize the difference between the emotional body and the inner self. It is helpful to affirm with conviction: "I have feelings, but I am not my feelings." And the final field of observation is that of mental activity, such as having various thoughts, beliefs, concepts, and attitudes. Because the inner self can observe, take notice, develop, and discipline the mind, it can be understood that the self is not the mind. Here it is helpful to affirm: "I have an intellect, but I am not my intellect." [22]

Second, apply the raja yoga technique discussed in chapter 2 by pondering or brooding over certain seed thoughts that can further self-observation. Pondering seed thoughts can be effective, because a life is changed primarily through reflection, characteristics are developed through directed thinking, and qualities are unfolded through deep consideration. The approach is to take a particular seed thought into the morning period of meditation, carrying out as best as can be done the various stages of raja yoga, and then to apply any new understanding to the rest of the day. For the purpose of cultivating the attitude of self-observation, Bailey recommends that the following seed thoughts be considered, with a different one used during each month for six months:

First month: I am the Observer, Who dwells ever at the centre.

Second month: I am the Interpreter, Who works ever from the centre.

Third month: I am the Desirer, Who draws all unto the centre.

Fourth month: I am the Dweller in the High Place, Who sees ever from the centre.

Fifth month: I am the Lover of men, Who pours
                      out love from the centre of love.

Sixth month: I am the Educator, Who, learning
                      myself at the centre, lifts thereto all
                      I seek to help.[23]

Third, each night before retiring, review the incidents, events, thoughts, words, and acts of the day. It is recommended that this evening review be done backward, beginning with the most recent events and then proceeding to the hour of rising. There is no need to take longer than ten or fifteen minutes because the effort is simply observing the incidents without dwelling on them. If it is inconvenient to do this review in the evening, because of fatigue or other duties, then it could be done at some other time. But it is best when this review is done regularly, once every twenty-four hours, and with care.[24]

And fourth, periodically step back and observe one's process of self-observation. To aid in this end, Bailey prepared a review on the attitude of the observer, which consists of the series of questions listed in Table 2. Detached self-observation is a power of the soul that works in association with the mind. Because there are seven types of souls, there are seven archetypal patterns of self-observation — one for each ray. Questions 17 and 18 in Table 2 indicate that it is possible to become aware of one's own pattern and the way that this pattern is expressed in daily life.

Character Building

The principal work of aspirants on the probationary path is to learn about themselves, ascertain their weaknesses, and then correct those weaknesses. In chapter 2, the probationary path was represented with two stages: self-observation, during which aspirants learn about themselves; and reorientation,

Table 2. Review on the Attitude of the Observer

---

1. What constitutes a review?
   a. Am I confusing a re-viewing with a re-doing or with a re-experiencing?
   b. Do I understand what I mean when I regard myself as an Observer?

2. What or who is the Observer? What is under observation?

3. Am I capable of learning to observe and of freeing myself from those results of observation which may not be desirable?

4. Can I observe myself mentally, unbiased by any reaction from the emotional personal self?

5. If I use this review on the attitude of the observer as it should be used,
   a. what will be the effect in my life?
   b. what will be the effect in the life of the group I wish to serve?

6. Can I honestly say that I can stand aside and observe with dispassion?

7. If this review work is a definitely scientific method of development, have I ever given the technique of observation a fair trial? Do I feel it now desirable? Why?

8. What basis can I find in my studies that this method of reviewing is the way for me, and that it will intensify my capacity for increased usefulness in service?

9. In what way can right observation speed my progress upon the Path?

10. If it is true that the blind must advance by *touching* but those with sight move forward by *seeing*, and by keeping free and unattached, why, then, having sight, do I close my eyes and fail to observe? What is the main hindrance?

11. Is my mind the organ of observation for the spiritual man? Can I offer this organ to the observer to use?

12. Can I hold my mind steady in the light which streams from the Observer? Can I hold it as the searchlight of the soul?

13. As I review today, what part has observation played?

14. How do I define the word "observation"?

15. Observation in the spiritual sense is a faculty which grows out of Self-realisation.
   a. Am I able to forget the fragmentary personal self?
   b. Can I centre my consciousness in the Self?

Table 2. Continued

16. Observation is a power of the Observer. It works in association with the mind. Do I understand and wield this power?

17. We are told that there is an archetype, a pattern, a ray, a goal and a light which reveals these higher patterns or divine ideas. Do I know anything of this? I mean, practically, in my daily life.

18. What is the archetypal pattern of observation, and how can it be expressed in my personal life?

19. Do I recognise and am I in touch with other Observers of the way of life?

20. Can I draw upon the power of observation and the wisdom of the Observer when others need it?

21. I am the redeemer of the lower nature. In what way does observation aid in this redemption?

22. Does redeeming force, released through observation, pour through me?

23. In what fashion will the observation of the Observer bring changes in my life, my habits, and my attitude?

24. Through which body do I most easily express myself? Which of my bodies requires the most observation and control?

25. Have I demonstrated the powers of observation today? Have I been in conscious contact at any moment with the Observer?

26. What activities and qualities of my lower nature (good as well as undesirable) need to be observed if I desire to serve more intelligently?

27. What is the major hindrance to my constant practice of observation? How can I offset this difficulty?

28. How does the assumption of the attitude of the Observer assist my fellowmen?

29. In what way can I most truly serve them? And how will observation help me to do this?

Source: A. A. Bailey, *Discipleship In the New Age*, vol. 1 (1944; reprint; New York: Lucis Publishing Company, 1976), 443–445.

during which they subordinate their weaknesses, or vices, and acquire the opposite qualities, or virtues. The stage of self-observation, which overlaps with all subsequent stages, was discussed in the last section. The stage of reorientation, often called character building, is considered next.

The terms *virtue* and *vice*, as they are used here, do not refer to conforming to various man-made laws and social customs. Rather, these terms refer to our attitude toward ourselves and toward our fellows. Virtue is the manifestation of the spirit of cooperation with others, implying unselfishness, understanding, and self-forgetfulness; whereas vice is the opposite of that attitude. Virtue is calling in the vibratory rhythm of group consciousness so that the soul becomes the controlling factor. Vice is the expression of a separative impulse that subordinates the soul to the goals of the lower self. Virtue is expressed through the heart chakra, whereas vice is expressed through the solar plexus chakra.

Through self-observation, careful reasoning, and evoking the wisdom of the soul, aspirants need to arrive at a truthful understanding of the vices that should be subordinated and the virtues that should be acquired. As discussed in chapter 2 and outlined in Table 3, each ray is associated with certain characteristic virtues, vices, and virtues to be acquired. An individual may have the virtues and vices associated with the rays of both the soul and the personality.

After discovering their strengths and weaknesses, how can aspirants reorient their lives? According to Bailey, "A vice is dominance of an involutionary quality of the same force which at a later period will show forth as a virtue." [25] Thus, each new virtue that is acquired is a transmutation of a corresponding vice. Rather than struggling with the vices, the effort of aspirants would be more effective if they persistently applied the new virtues, which automatically weaken the vices. The approach is to develop new habit patterns and initiate new forms of constructive activity while no longer feeding the old patterns and allowing those patterns to fall into decay through

Table 3. Virtues and Vices Associated with the Seven Rays

Ray	Special Virtues	Vices	Virtues to Be Acquired
One	Strength, courage, steadfastness, truthfulness arising from absolute fearlessness, power of ruling, capacity to grasp great questions in a large-minded way, and of handling men and measures	Pride, ambition, willfulness, hardness, arrogance, desire to control others, obstinacy, anger	Tenderness, humility, sympathy, tolerance, patience
Two	Calm, strength, patience and endurance, love of truth, faithfulness, intuition, clear intelligence, and serene temper	Overabsorption in study, coldness, indifference to others, contempt of mental limitations in others	Love, compassion, unselfishness, energy
Three	Wide views on all abstract questions, sincerity of purpose, clear intellect, capacity	Intellectual pride, coldness, isolation, inaccuracy in details, absent-mindedness,	Sympathy, tolerance, devotion, accuracy, energy and common sense

Table 3. Continued

Ray	Special Virtues	Vices	Virtues to Be Acquired
	for concentration on philosophic studies, patience, caution, absence to the tendency to worry himself or others over trifles	obstinacy, selfishness, overmuch criticism of others	
Four	Strong affections, sympathy, physical courage, generosity, devotion, quickness of intellect and perception	Self-centeredness, worrying, inaccuracy, lack of moral courage, strong passions, indolence, extravagance	Serenity, confidence, self-control, purity, unselfishness, accuracy, mental and moral balance
Five	Strictly accurate statements, justice (without mercy), perseverance, common sense, uprightness, independence, keen intellect	Harsh criticism, narrowness, arrogance, unforgiving temper, lack of sympathy and reverence, prejudice	Reverence, devotion, sympathy, love, wide-mindedness

Table 3. Continued

Ray	Special Virtues	Vices	Virtues to Be Acquired
Six	Devotion, single-mindedness, love, tenderness, intuition, loyalty, reverence	Selfish and jealous love, overleaning on others, partiality, self-deception, sectarianism, superstition, prejudice, overrapid conclusions, fiery anger	Strength, self-sacrifice, purity, truth, tolerance, serenity, balance and common sense
Seven	Strength, perseverance, courage, extreme care in details, self-reliance, courtesy	Formalism, bigotry, pride, narrowness, superficial judgments, self-opinion overindulged	Realisation of unity, wide-mindedness, tolerance, humility, gentleness and love

Source: A. A. Bailey, *Esoteric Psychology*, vol. 1 (1936; reprint; New York: Lucis Publishing Company, 1975), 201–210.

lack of attention. The key to progress is self-effort combined with a conscious comprehension of the work to be done.

Next, three suggestions are given on how to facilitate this process of character building. First, use what Bailey calls the "Technique of Indifference." The word *indifference* implies that no undue attention is paid to the vices. However, Bailey uses this word in a stronger sense: there is an attitude of actively repudiating the vices but without focusing any concentration on them. This type of repudiation is based on recognizing the basic distinction between the spiritual "self," which expresses virtues, and the "not-self," which expresses vices. It requires a constant recollection of the truth of being the spiritual self and a refusal to be identified with anything except that spiritual self.[26]

Second, apply the raja yoga technique by pondering the virtues that need to be acquired. It is recommended that only one virtue be considered during each day and that the same virtue be considered for one month. Because each virtue is an expression of a quality of the soul, it can be interpreted esoterically and in terms of relationships. While many thoughts and ideas may come that are well known and commonplace, each virtue has deeper meanings that are of real importance and are generally unknown to the average person. The goal of this meditation is to find those deeper meanings. At the end of each month, as a way of summarizing and making concrete the learning that has occurred, it is recommended that a short paper be written on the virtue that was considered during that month.[27]

And third, during a daily meditation period, use visualization to picture yourself as the ideal person. Start by imagining yourself as the exponent of the virtue that is most desired, and then add virtue to virtue until all of the virtues have been included. During the rest of the day, attempt to become the visualized picture in daily life. In this way, a definite mental thoughtform is being built that can be used to step out of a lower state of consciousness into a higher one.[28]

As shown in the next section, visualization can be used for purposes other than acquiring new virtues. Visualization is an important skill to master because when done effectively it can demonstrate the truth of the occult law that "energy follows thought." The visualization of pictures tends to focus the meditator within the head at a point midway between the pituitary gland and the pineal gland. In that area, one draws the pictures and paints the scenes representing what one desires and what one intends to work for. The creative imagination is used to picture a form, and the thought energy of the mind gives life and direction to that form. As a result, a rapport is established between the mind and the emotional body. When it is desired to change long-standing habit patterns, the energy of will or intention can be gathered by the power of visualization into the area surrounding the pineal gland, which then can be directed to affect the subconscious mind and etheric body. This use of visualization is a technique of magic because it enables a mental image to be manifested tangibly in the physical world. When the wisdom of the soul guides this process, it is a technique of white magic.[29]

Emotional Purification

During the path of probation, aspirants model their lives according to their *theory* of what virtuous behavior is like. They attempt to create a structure of right thinking and right conduct. When they succeed in making that theory part of themselves, the heart chakra becomes developed, marking the completion of the path of probation and the attainment of the first initiation. The structure that has been built is no longer dormant but has become alive, because they have attained a higher state of consciousness. They are now ready to begin a new phase of the spiritual path called the path of discipleship. During this new phase, disciples become increasingly sensitive to the intuitive voice of the soul. As shown in chapter 2, the guidance given by the soul varies depending on the ray of the soul. For all rays, however, they are guided to purify their emotional lives by discovering and deliberately eliminating their glamours. We will consider this process of purification in detail.

Glamour can be defined as being an emotional reaction that prevents clear perception. Its effect can be likened to a mist or fog that distorts everything that is seen or contacted, preventing the surrounding conditions from being seen as they essentially are. Because glamour enters the mind through familiar habits of thought, it is frequently present. Because of the nature of sentient reactions, it is powerful. And by being able to masquerade as the truth, it is subtle.

Before a glamour can be eradicated, it first has to be discovered through self-observation. However, we generally do not recognize glamour when it meets and envelops us. At the beginning of the effort of self-observation, we can infer the presence of a glamour from its effects; for instance, glamour is present whenever there is pride, self-pity, or criticism. Later, when our process of observation is sufficiently advanced, we can recognize the true nature of a glamour before being immersed and deluded by it.

Table 4 on pages 114–116 lists some of the glamours associated with each of the seven ray types. Generally there are two sets of glamours. By taking pride in one's method of accomplishment, one has glamours associated with the soul ray; and by taking pride in one's area of application, one has glamours associated with the personality ray.

It is important to distinguish between glamour and illusion. An illusion is a false belief or opinion that dominates and distorts thinking. It could be based on a traditional idea from the past, an idea from a current ideology, or a dimly sensed idea that will become popular in the future. Whenever there is a real grasp of the whole idea, there can be no illusion. But if that idea is wrongly perceived, wrongly interpreted, or wrongly appropriated, then it can become a narrow and sepa-

Table 4. Glamours Associated with the Seven Rays

Ray One

The glamour of physical strength
The glamour of personal magnetism
The glamour of self-centeredness and personal potency
The glamour of "the one at the centre"
The glamour of selfish personal ambition
The glamour of rulership, of dictatorship and of wide control
The glamour of the Messiah complex in the field of politics
The glamour of selfish destiny, of the divine right of kings
  personally exacted
The glamour of destruction
The glamour of isolation, of aloneness, of aloofness
The glamour of the superimposed will—upon others and upon groups

Ray Two

The glamour of the love of being loved
The glamour of popularity
The glamour of personal wisdom
The glamour of selfish responsibility
The glamour of too complete an understanding, which negates
  right action
The glamour of self-pity, a basic glamour of this ray
The glamour of the Messiah complex, in the world of religion
  and world need
The glamour of fear, based on undue sensitivity
The glamour of self-sacrifice
The glamour of selfish unselfishness
The glamour of self-satisfaction
The glamour of selfish service

Ray Three

The glamour of being busy
The glamour of cooperation with the Plan in an individual and
  not a group way
The glamour of active scheming
The glamour of creative work—without true motive
The glamour of good intentions, which are basically selfish
The glamour of "the spider at the centre"
The glamour of "God in the machine"
The glamour of devious and continuous manipulation
The glamour of self-importance, from the standpoint of
  knowing, of efficiency

Table 4. Continued

Ray Four

The glamour of harmony, aiming at personal comfort and satisfaction
The glamour of war
The glamour of conflict, with the objective of imposing
  righteousness and peace
The glamour of vague artistic perception
The glamour of psychic perception instead of intuition.
The glamour of musical perception
The glamour of the pairs of opposites, in the higher sense

Ray Five

The glamour of materially, or overemphasis of form
The glamour of the intellect
The glamour of knowledge and of definition
The glamour of assurance, based on a narrow point of view
The glamour of the form which hides reality
The glamour of organisation
The glamour of the outer, which hides the inner

Ray Six

The glamour of devotion
The glamour of adherence to forms and persons
The glamour of idealism
The glamour of loyalties, of creeds
The glamour of emotional response
The glamour of sentimentality
The glamour of interference
The glamour of the lower pairs of opposites
The glamour of World Saviours and Teachers
The glamour of the narrow vision
The glamour of fanaticism

Ray Seven

The glamour of magical work
The glamour of the relation of the opposites
The glamour of the subterranean powers
The glamour of that which brings together
The glamour of the physical body
The glamour of the mysterious and the secret
The glamour of sex magic
The glamour of the emerging manifested forces

Source: A. A. Bailey, *Glamour: A World Problem* (1950; reprint; New York: Lucis
Publishing Company, 1971), 120–123.

rative ideal, resulting in illusion. Because of illusion, people become fanatics, sadistic enforcers of narrow ideals, and limited visionaries.

For example, the idea that finds expression in the statement "all men are equal" is a fact and not an illusion. But that idea becomes an illusion when it is translated into an ideal that makes no allowance for the equally important ideas of evolution, racial attributes, and national characteristics. As another example, each of the major ideological systems of our modern times — including democracy, capitalism, and communism — was originally based on a true idea that was later translated into an illusion in the form of an enforced ideal. In a professed effort to help the poor and the backward, proponents of each of these systems have assassinated leaders, burned villages, terrorized populations, and violated all standards of decency.[30]

While glamour is an emotional distortion, illusion is a mental distortion. While glamour is the major problem that must be solved by a disciple between the first and second initiations, illusion is the major problem that must be solved between the second and third initiations. The method of dissipating glamour is different from that used for dispelling illusion. It is the illumined mind that dissipates glamour. And it is the soul itself, through using the faculties of wisdom and insight, that dispels illusion.

Next, a systematic method for dissipating glamour is described that augments the raja yoga technique with certain visualizations and affirmations. It is recommended that this method be applied to the particular glamour that is most apparent and hindering. After that glamour is dissipated, subtler glamours will be recognized, which in their turn also must be eradicated. This method has ten steps and is an adaptation of some instructions called the "Technique of Light" that were originally given by Bailey.[31]

First, recognize the particular glamour that has been chosen for dissipation. Identify the ways in which this glamour distorts perception or reality, affects daily life, and hinders right relationships.

Second, by using the power of creative imagination, visualize the threefold lower self (physical, emotional, and mental) as being coordinated and functioning as a single unified whole.

Third, visualize the soul as sending the lights of wisdom and insight to the mental body of the attentive waiting personality.

Fourth, visualize the mental body combining its own light of knowledge with the lights of wisdom and insight so that these three lights are fused and blended. See this one unified light as generating a searchlight of great brilliance and strength but one that is not yet projecting outward.

Fifth, use the power of visualization to gather the energy of will or intention, and then focus this energy behind the visualized searchlight. Although the will is dynamic, at this stage it is quiescent.

Sixth, use the raja yoga technique to relate the searchlight of the mind to the specific glamour selected for dissipation. As best you can, carry out the stages of concentration and meditation, which involves using the mind to analyze the glamour while being guided by the soul. The goal is to achieve a realization of the essential nature of the glamour, including its cause and meaning. When this realization is attained, the glamour is appreciably weakened.

Seventh, after achieving the needed realization as far as possible, use creative imagination to project the searchlight of the mind. See a vivid beam of light streaming forth and piercing the glamour.

Eighth, while visualizing the glamour as being pierced, aid the process by saying the following affirmations: "The power of the light prevents the appearance of the glamour (naming it)"; "The power of the light negates the quality of the glamour from affecting me"; and "The power of the light destroys the life behind the glamour." Say these affirmations at a point of tension, with the mind held in steadiness and having a positive orientation.

Ninth, visualize the light as penetrating the glamour, being absorbed by the glamour, and finally dissipating the glamour.

And tenth, visualize the beam of light as being withdrawn back to the mental body. Be focused in the mental body, knowing that the work has been successfully carried forward, and relinquish all thought of the glamour.

The foregoing method is not a process of "killing out desire" through the use of suppression but is a process of gradually eradicating selfish desire through the illumination of the mind. Selfish desire can be viewed as the urge of the personality toward betterment, and it is a definite asset at the right time and place. However, it has to be gradually transformed in order for the personality to become an instrument of the soul.

In this method, the essential and necessary step is number six, which uses the discipline of raja yoga to illuminate the mind regarding the particular glamour being considered. The purpose of the preceding steps of visualization is to assist in attaining the necessary alignment between the mental body and soul. The purpose of the subsequent steps of visualization and affirmation is to bring the energy of illumination down through the emotional body to affect the subconscious mind and etheric body. Through the combination of these techniques of raja yoga and white magic, significant changes can be made in long-standing habitual patterns of thought, feeling, and activity.

Service

Each initiation constitutes an expansion of consciousness that marks the transition from one point of polarization to another. To attain the first initiation, the aspirant must demonstrate physical control, which means being able to display virtuous behavior. To attain the second initiation, the disciple must demonstrate emotional control, which requires knowing how glamours can be eradicated through the illumination of the mind. To attain the third initiation, one must demonstrate mental control, which means that the soul itself assumes the dominant position and directs the mind.

After the second initiation, self-centeredness may continue to play a potent part in the lives of disciples, and their old desires may at times still dominate. They continue with their earlier disciplines of evoking the guidance of the soul, practicing self-observation, and dissipating glamours. In addition, as discussed in chapter 2, they learn to practice the method of occult meditation that is appropriate for their ray, which involves becoming temporarily polarized in the realm of abstract thought or the soul. Through this meditation, they are able to dispel their illusions and render true service. The nature of that service is considered next.

Having the ability to be a true server signifies an advanced stage of development on the spiritual path. Until that stage has been reached, it is not possible to perform spontaneous service that is guided by wisdom, motivated by inclusive love, and provided without attachment. What is found instead is a combination of good intentions, mixed motives, and often fanaticism. It may be helpful to list some of these lesser forms of service. Servers who have found their ideas to be true, useful, and good may believe that their ideas are necessarily good for everyone and render service with the motive of bringing others to the same viewpoint. Servers who are made uncomfortable by distressing conditions may provide service to the poor, the diseased, and the unhappy, so that the servers themselves will be made more comfortable. Service may be given out of a sense of obedience, to either a human or a divine authority, rather than as a spontaneous outgoing toward the needy. If service is regarded as a qualification for discipleship, then it may be performed out of a desire for spiritual perfection. Service may be given because it has become fashionable and customary. It may provide a sense of power, an opportunity to feel superior toward and dominate those who are being served. And service may be given with the motive of meeting new friends, because it is generally a group activity.[32]

The foregoing list shows that much of the service being rendered today is distorted by the glamours of the servers. Because of their emotional identification with the suffering and the blame they lay on others for the distressing conditions, today's servers often have an intense hatred. Instead of a real understanding and true helpfulness, there often is busyness, ambition, and a love of power. Nevertheless, such service may be a step forward on the server's own evolutionary path, and it may provide significant material assistance to those being served.

In contrast, true service is neither a sentiment nor an ideal. It is neither an activity toward which people must strive, nor a method for helping others. Instead, true service can be defined as being the spontaneous effect of soul contact. Service is the outstanding characteristic of the soul, just as selfish desire is the outstanding characteristic of the personality. Service can be regarded as an instinct of the soul, just as the urge to reproduce is an instinct of the animal nature. From this point of view, true service can neither be taught nor be imposed on another person. Rather, the ability to serve is gained through contact with the soul, and it is the evidence that the soul is beginning to express itself in outer manifestation.[33]

The various stages of the spiritual path can be viewed as stages of preparation for a life of service. By progressing through these stages, the disciple's service becomes distinguished by the following qualities. First, there will be harmlessness, or an active refraining from those acts and speech that might hurt or cause misunderstanding. Second, there will be a willingness to let others serve as seems best to them. And third, by experiencing the rhythms of the soul, there will be joyfulness.[34]

As inner contact with the soul becomes more frequent, the disciple's life of meditation deepens. By reaching a stage wherein the mind is sufficiently poised and peaceful, one can receive intuitively the new ideas associated with the next step to be taken in world evolution, as well as learn the part one may play in that evolutionary process. That part generally includes contacting those individuals who are at a point in their personal evolution where they can respond to these new ideas but who are not yet sufficiently intuitive to receive the ideas directly for themselves. As discussed next, workers on each ray have their own distinctive method of rendering this service.

Servers on the first ray use their powerful will to make an impact on the minds of their listeners, which is done by emphasizing the governing principles that are to be assimilated next by humanity. These servers initiate a period of destruction, breaking up the old forms of truth and making room for the new emerging ideas.

After pondering and assimilating the new ideas, servers on the second ray use the power of their attractive love to gather together students who can respond to these ideas in some measure. They then teach and train those students, who in turn carry the new ideas deeper into the mass of humanity.

Servers on the third ray manipulate and adapt the new ideas in order to facilitate their comprehension by intelligent men and women. Through their speeches, books, and articles, they help to stimulate and inspire the intellect of humanity.

Servers on the fourth ray have the task of harmonizing the new ideas with the old so that there is no dangerous break. Through this synthesis, they are able to bring forth a true presentation of the complete picture.

Using scientific investigation, servers on the fifth ray have the task of examining new hypotheses and proving them as either true or false. Afterwards, they communicate their findings to the scientific community by formulating new theories, principles, experiments, or mechanical contrivances, which in due time are understood and utilized by the rest of the world.

Servers on the sixth ray help train the world thinkers to ardently desire the good, the true, and the beautiful, and in particular to desire those ideals whose time has come to be manifested on earth. These servers steadily uphold the ideals to be manifested while being careful to restrain their listeners from being too fanatical.

Servers on the seventh ray help through organizing activities on the physical plane. Their work is to transform group aspiration for a particular ideal into an organized movement, without allowing any one individual to dominate that movement.[35]

In summary, true service is not simply an activity of some person or group doing something with good intention for another person or group. Rather, service is an outer effect of inner contact with the soul, and it is the natural expression of the life of the soul. The line of least resistance and greatest efficiency is the form and direction determined by the ray of the server's soul. Because there are seven rays, there are seven distinctive methods in service, and all of these methods work together to produce a single synthetic whole.

Notes

Introduction

1. H. P. Blavatsky, *The Secret Doctrine*, vol. 1 (1888; reprint; Pasadena, CA: Theosophical University Press, 1977), 573.
2. E. Wood, *The Seven Rays* (1925; reprint; Wheaton, IL: Theosophical Publishing House, 1984).
3. G. Hodson, *The Seven Human Temperaments* (1952; reprint; Adyar, India: Theosophical Publishing House, 1981).
4. A. A. Bailey, *A Treatise on the Seven Rays*, in 5 vols: *Esoteric Psychology*, vol. 1 (1936; reprint; New York: Lucis Publishing Company, 1975); *Esoteric Psychology*, vol. 2 (1942; reprint; New York: Lucis Publishing Company, 1975); *Esoteric Astrology* (1951; reprint; New York: Lucis Publishing Company, 1977); *Esoteric Healing* (1953; reprint; New York: Lucis Publishing Company, 1977); and *The Rays and the Initiations* (1960; reprint; New York: Lucis Publishing Company, 1976).
5. M. J. Eastcott, *The Seven Rays of Energy* (Kent, England: Sundial House, 1980); K. Abraham, *Introduction to the Seven Rays* (Cape May, NJ: Lampus Press, 1986); H. S.

Burmester, *The Seven Rays Made Visual* (Marina Del Ray, CA: DeVorss and Company, 1986).

6. R. Assagioli, *Psychosynthesis Typology* (London: Institute of Psychosynthesis, 1983).

7. D. C. Tansley, *Chakras — Rays and Radionics* (Essex, England: C. W. Daniel Company Limited, 1983); Z. F. Lansdowne, *The Chakras and Esoteric Healing* (York Beach, ME: Samuel Weiser, Inc., 1986), 93–101.

8. *The Journal of Esoteric Psychology*, vol. 3 (Jersey City Heights, NJ: The Seven Ray Institute, 1987).

9. Bailey, *Esoteric Psychology*, vol. 2, 378.

10. H. Chaudhuri, *Integral Yoga* (1965; reprint; San Francisco: California Institute of Asian Studies, 1970), 21–22.

11. A. A. Bailey, *Glamour: A World Problem* (1950; reprint; New York: Lucis Publishing Company, 1971), 6–14.

12. Bailey, *Esoteric Psychology*, vol. 1, 112.

Chapter 1: The Seven Rays

1. A. A. Bailey, *A Treatise On White Magic* (1934; reprint; New York: Lucis Publishing Company, 1974), 393–398; A. A. Bailey, *Esoteric Psychology*, vol. 2 (1942; reprint; New York: Lucis Publishing Company, 1975), 336–337.

2. Bailey, *Esoteric Psychology*, vol. 2, 36.

3. Bailey, *Esoteric Psychology*, vol. 2, 36.

4. A. A. Bailey, *Esoteric Psychology*, vol. 1 (1936; reprint; New York: Lucis Publishing Company, 1975), 201–202.

5. Bailey, *Esoteric Psychology*, vol. 2, 77–79.

6. A. A. Bailey, *A Treatise on Cosmic Fire* (1925; reprint; New York: Lucis Publishing Company, 1973), 538–544, 816–829.

7. Bailey, *Esoteric Psychology*, vol. 2, 36.

8. Bailey, *Esoteric Psychology*, vol. 1, 202–204.

9. Bailey, *Esoteric Psychology*, vol. 2, 37.

10. Bailey, *Esoteric Psychology*, vol. 1, 204–205.

11. A. A. Bailey, *Glamour: A World Problem* (1950; reprint; New York: Lucis Publishing Company, 1971), 21–22, 26.

12. Bailey, *Glamour: A World Problem*, 222.

13. A. A. Bailey, *Education in the New Age* (1954; reprint; New York: Lucis Publishing Company, 1974), 147; A. A. Bailey, *Esoteric Healing* (1953; reprint; New York: Lucis Publishing Company, 1977), 72.

14. Bailey, *Esoteric Psychology*, vol. 2, 37.

15. Bailey, *Esoteric Psychology*, vol. 1, 205–207.

16. Bailey, *A Treatise on White Magic*, 228–229; Bailey, *Esoteric Psychology*, vol. 2, 162–163.

17. H. Chaudhuri, *Integral Yoga* (1965; reprint; San Francisco: California Institute of Asian Studies, 1970), 53–54.

18. Bailey, *Esoteric Psychology*, vol. 2, 37–38.

19. Bailey, *Esoteric Psychology*, vol. 1, 207–208.

20. Z. F. Lansdowne, *The Chakras and Esoteric Healing* (York Beach, ME: Samuel Weiser, Inc., 1986), 7–8.

21. Bailey, *Esoteric Psychology*, vol. 2, 38.

22. Bailey, *Esoteric Psychology*, vol. 1, 208–210.

23. A. A. Bailey, *Telepathy and the Etheric Vehicle* (1950; reprint; New York: Lucis Publishing Company, 1975), 146; Bailey, *Esoteric Healing*, 461.

24. Bailey, *Esoteric Psychology*, vol. 2, 38–39.

25. Bailey, *Esoteric Psychology*, vol. 1, 210–211.

26. Bailey, *A Treatise on Cosmic Fire*, 977–982; Bailey, *Glamour: A World Problem*, 222.

27. A. A. Bailey, *The Destiny of The Nations* (1949; reprint; New York: Lucis Publishing Company, 1974), 123.

Chapter 2: Techniques of Integration

1. A. A. Bailey, *Esoteric Healing* (1953; reprint; New York: Lucis Publishing Company, 1977), 186–187, 202; A. A. Bailey, *A Treatise on White Magic* (1934; reprint; New York: Lucis Publishing Company, 1974), 591–592.

2. Z. F. Lansdowne, *The Chakras and Esoteric Healing* (York Beach, ME: Samuel Weiser, Inc. 1986), 29–39.

3. A. A. Bailey, *Esoteric Psychology*, vol. 2 (1942; reprint; New York: Lucis Publishing Company, 1975), 351–352.

4. A. A. Bailey, *Discipleship in the New Age*, vol. 1 (1944; New York: Lucis Publishing Company, 1976), 494; Bailey, *A Treatise on White Magic*, 558.

5. A. A. Bailey, *Letters on Occult Meditation* (1922; reprint; New York: Lucis Publishing Company, 1974), 348–349.

6. Bailey, *A Treatise on White Magic*, 585–586.

7. Bailey, *A Treatise on White Magic*, 586–587.

8. A. A. Bailey, *Glamour: A World Problem* (1950; reprint; New York: Lucis Publishing Company, 1971), 80, 120–121.

9. Bailey, *Esoteric Psychology*, vol. 2, 391–392.

10. Bailey, *Esoteric Psychology*, vol. 2, 392–393.

11. Swami Nikhilananda, *The Bhagavad Gita* (1944; reprint; New York: Ramakrishna-Vivekananda Center, 1969), 88–89.

12. Bailey, *Esoteric Psychology*, vol. 2, 355.

13. Bailey, *Glamour: A World Problem*, 76–77.

14. Bailey, *Glamour: A World Problem*, 121, 222–223.

15. Bailey, *A Treatise on White Magic*, 585.

16. Bailey, *Esoteric Psychology*, vol. 2, 482.

17. Bailey, *A Treatise on White Magic*, 584–585.

18. Bailey, *Letters on Occult Meditation*, 285–286.

19. Bailey, *Glamour: A World Problem*, 180; Bailey, *Discipleship in the New Age*, vol. 1, 390–393.

20. Bailey, *Glamour: A World Problem*, 171.

21. *A Course in Miracles*, vol. 1 (Tiburon, CA: Foundation for Inner Peace, 1975), 24.

22. Sri Aurobindo, *The Synthesis of Yoga* (Pondicherry, India: Sri Aurobindo Ashram, 1957), 41–42; H. Chaudhuri, *Integral Yoga* (1965; San Francisco: California Institute of Asian Studies, 1970), 62–65.

23. Bailey, *Esoteric Psychology*, vol. 2, 360.

24. Bailey, *Discipleship in the New Age*, vol. 1, 83–84.

25. Bailey, *Glamour: A World Problem*, 121–122, 144–145.

26. Bailey, *Letters on Occult Meditation*, 16.

27. N. Thera, *The Heart of Buddhist Meditation* (1962; reprint; York Beach, ME: Samuel Weiser, Inc., 1973), 30–54.

28. Bailey, *Esoteric Psychology*, vol. 2, 363.

29. Bailey, *Glamour: A World Problem*, 79.

30. R. Fisher and W. Ury, *Getting to Yes: How to Negotiate Agreement Without Giving In* (Boston: Houghton Mifflin, 1981); D. G. Pruitt, "Achieving Integrative Agreements in Negotiation," in *Negotiating in Organizations*, edited by M. H. Bazerman and R. J. Lewicki (Beverly Hills, CA: Sage, 1983), 35–50.

31. J. Marks and B. Pearlman, "Beyond Protest: Common Ground," *New Options*, no. 22 (Washington, DC: New Options, Inc., 1985), 1–2; T. Brown, "The New Activism: Forging Consensus," *New Options*, no. 22 (Washington, DC: New Options, Inc., 1985), 2.

32. Bailey, *Esoteric Psychology*, vol. 2, 368–369.

33. A. A. Bailey, *The Light of the Soul* (1927; reprint; New York: Lucis Trust, 1978), 243–250.

34. Bailey, *A Treatise on White Magic*, 14–16, 333.

35. A. A. Bailey, *From Intellect to Intuition* (1932; reprint; New York: Lucis Publishing Company, 1974), 113, 132–144; Bailey, *Glamour: A World Problem*, 6–14.

36. Bailey, *Glamour: A World Problem*, 223.

37. Bailey, *Letters on Occult Meditation*, 17–18.

38. Bailey, *From Intellect to Intuition*, 98–99.

39. Bailey, *Esoteric Psychology*, vol. 2, 371–372.

40. A. A. Bailey, *Discipleship in the New Age*, vol. 2 (1955; reprint; New York: Lucis Publishing Company, 1972), 490, 641–642.

41. Bailey, *Letters on Occult Meditation*, 121–122.

42. Bailey, *Glamour: A World Problem*, 77–78, 123.

43. Bailey, *Esoteric Psychology*, vol. 2, 600–601.

44. Bailey, *Glamour: A World Problem*, 221–223.

45. Bailey, *Letters on Occult Meditation*, 18.

46. Swami Vivekananda, "Bhakti-Yoga," in *The Yogas and Other Works* (New York: Ramakrishna-Vivekananda Center, 1953), 433.

47. P. Yogananda, *Autobiography of a Yogi* (1946; reprint; Los Angeles: Self-Realization Fellowship, 1969).

48. Bailey, *Esoteric Psychology*, vol. 2, 375–376.

49. E. Holmes, *The Science of Mind* (New York: Dodd, Mead and Company, 1938).

50. Bailey, *Esoteric Psychology*, vol. 2, 133–134; Bailey, *Discipleship in the New Age*, vol. 2, 391–392.

51. Bailey, *Esoteric Psychology*, vol. 2, 135–136; Bailey, *Discipleship in the New Age*, vol. 1, 25.

52. A. A. Bailey, *A Treatise on Cosmic Fire* (1925; reprint; New York: Lucis Publishing Company, 1977), 817.

53. Bailey, *A Treatise on White Magic*, 515–516.

54. Bailey, *A Treatise on White Magic*, 518–519.

55. Bailey, *A Treatise on White Magic*, 551–552.

56. M. P. Hall, *Magic* (Los Angeles: Philosophical Research Society, 1978), 46; E. Levi, *Transcendental Magic* (1896; reprint; London: Rider and Company, 1984), 237.

57. Bailey, *Esoteric Psychology*, vol. 2, 371.

Chapter 3: Applications

1. A. A. Bailey, *Esoteric Psychology*, vol. 2 (1942; reprint; New York: Lucis Publishing Company, 1975), 427–428.

2. Bailey, *Esoteric Psychology*, vol. 2, 417–421.

3. Bailey, *Esoteric Psychology*, vol. 2, 428–429.

4. Bailey, *Esoteric Psychology*, vol. 2, 421–423.

5. Bailey, *Esoteric Psychology*, vol. 2, 423–424.

6. Bailey, *Esoteric Psychology*, vol. 2, 357.

7. Bailey, *Esoteric Psychology*, vol. 2, 445–447, 498–499.

8. P. Yogananda, *Autobiography of a Yogi* (1946; reprint; Los Angeles: Self-Realization Fellowship, 1969), 332.

9. A. A. Bailey, *Letters on Occult Meditation* (1922; reprint; New York: Lucis Publishing Company, 1974), 19; Bailey, *Esoteric Psychology*, vol. 2, 358.

10. Bailey, *Letters on Occult Meditation*, 19–21, 107–109.

11. A. A. Bailey, *Esoteric Psychology*, vol. 1 (1936; reprint; New York: Lucis Publishing Company, 1975), 406.

12. Bailey, *Letters on Occult Meditation*, 20–21.

13. Bailey, *Esoteric Psychology*, vol. 2, 335.

14. Bailey, *Esoteric Psychology*, vol. 2, 303.

15. A. A. Bailey, *The Destiny of the Nations* (1949; New York: Lucis Publishing Company, 1974), 45; A. A. Bailey, *The Externalisation of the Hierarchy* (1957; reprint; New York: Lucis Publishing Company, 1976), 10.

16. Bailey, *Esoteric Psychology*, vol. 2, 480–485.

17. Bailey, *Esoteric Psychology*, vol. 2, 482–483.

18. Bailey, *Esoteric Psychology*, vol. 2, 486.

19. Bailey, *Esoteric Psychology*, vol. 2, 488–491.

20. Bailey, *Esoteric Psychology*, vol. 2, 489–491.

21. A. A. Bailey, *A Treatise on White Magic* (1934; reprint; New York: Lucis Publishing Company, 1974), 179–180; Bailey, *Letters on Occult Meditation*, 292–293.

22. R. Assagioli, *Psychosynthesis* (1965; reprint; New York; Penguin Books, 1987), 111–120.

23. A. A. Bailey, *Discipleship in the New Age*, vol. 1 (1944; reprint; New York: Lucis Publishing Company, 1976), 443.

24. Bailey, *Discipleship in the New Age*, vol. 1, 194.

25. Bailey, *Letters on Occult Meditation*, 233.

26. A. A. Bailey, *Glamour: A World Problem* (1950; reprint; New York: Lucis Publishing Company, 1971), 262–263.
27. A. A. Bailey, *Discipleship in the New Age*, vol. 2 (1955; reprint; New York: Lucis Publishing Company, 1972), 660–661.
28. Bailey, *Letters on Occult Meditation*, 146.
29. Bailey, *Discipleship in the New Age*, vol. 1, 89–91.
30. Bailey, *Glamour: A World Problem*, 132.
31. Bailey, *Glamour: A World Problem*, 215–219.
32. Bailey, *Esoteric Psychology*, vol. 2, 119–122.
33. Bailey, *Esoteric Psychology*, vol. 2, 124–125.
34. Bailey, *Esoteric Psychology*, vol. 2, 131–133.
35. Bailey, *Esoteric Psychology*, vol. 2, 140–145.

Bibliography

Abraham, K. B. *Introduction to the Seven Rays*. Cape May, NJ: Lampus Press, 1986.

Assagioli, R. *Psychosynthesis*. 1965. Reprint. New York: Penguin Books, 1987.

_____. *Psychosynthesis Typology*. London: Institute of Psychosynthesis, 1983.

Aurobindo, Sri. *The Synthesis of Yoga*. Pondicherry, India: Sri Aurobindo Ashram, 1957.

Bailey, A. A. *The Destiny of the Nations*. 1949. Reprint. New York: Lucis Publishing Company, 1974.

_____. *Discipleship in the New Age*, vol. 1. 1944. Reprint. New York: Lucis Publishing Company, 1976.

_____. *Discipleship in the New Age*, vol. 2. 1955. Reprint. New York: Lucis Publishing Company, 1972.

_____. *Education in the New Age*. 1954. Reprint. New York: Lucis Publishing Company, 1974.

_____. *Esoteric Astrology*. 1951. Reprint. New York: Lucis Publishing Company, 1979.

_____. *Esoteric Healing*. 1953. Reprint. New York: Lucis Publishing Company, 1977.

_____. *Esoteric Psychology*, vol. 1. 1936. Reprint. New York: Lucis Publishing Company, 1975.

———. *Esoteric Psychology*, vol. 2. 1942. Reprint. New York: Lucis Publishing Company, 1975.

———. *The Externalisation of the Hierarchy*. 1957. Reprint. New York: Lucis Publishing Company, 1976.

———. *From Intellect to Intuition*. 1932. Reprint. New York: Lucis Publishing Company, 1974.

———. *Glamour: A World Problem*. 1950. Reprint. New York: Lucis Publishing Company, 1971.

———. *Letters on Occult Meditation*. 1922. Reprint. New York: Lucis Publishing Company, 1974.

———. *The Light of the Soul*. 1955. Reprint. New York: Lucis Publishing Company, 1978.

———. *The Rays and the Initiations*. 1960. Reprint. New York: Lucis Publishing Company, 1976.

———. *Telepathy and the Etheric Vehicle*. 1950. Reprint. New York: Lucis Publishing Company, 1975.

———. *A Treatise on Cosmic Fire*. 1925. Reprint. New York: Lucis Publishing Company, 1977.

———. *A Treatise on White Magic*. 1934. Reprint. New York: Lucis Publishing Company, 1974.

Blavatsky, H. P. *The Secret Doctrine*. 1888. Reprint. Pasadena, CA: Theosophical University Press, 1977.

Brown, T. "The New Activism: Forging Consensus," *New Options*, no. 22. Washington, DC: New Options, Inc, 1985.

Burmester, H. S. *The Seven Rays Made Visual*. Marina Del Ray, CA: DeVorss and Company, 1986.

Chaudhuri, H. *Integral Yoga*. 1965. Reprint. San Francisco: California Institute of Asian Studies, 1970.

A Course in Miracles, vols. 1, 2, 3. Tiburon, CA: Foundation for Inner Peace, 1975.

Creme, B. *Maitreya's Mission*. Amsterdam: Share International Foundation, 1986.

Eastcott, M. J. *The Seven Rays of Energy*. Kent, England: Sundial House, 1980.

Fisher, R., and W. Ury. *Getting to Yes: How to Negotiate Agreement Without Giving In*. Boston: Houghton Mifflin, 1981.

Hall, M. P. *Magic*. Los Angeles: Philosophical Research Society, 1978.

Hodson, G. *The Seven Human Temperaments*. 1952. Reprint. Adyar, India: Theosophical Publishing House, 1981.

Holmes, E. *The Science of Mind*. New York: Dodd, Mead and Company, 1938.

The Journal of Esoteric Psychology, vol. 3. Jersey City Heights, NJ: The Seven Ray Institute, 1987.

Lansdowne, Z. F. *The Chakras and Esoteric Healing*. York Beach, ME: Samuel Weiser, Inc. 1986.

Levi, E. *Transcendental Magic*. 1896. Reprint. London: Rider and Company, 1984.

Marks, J., and B. Pearlman. "Beyond Protest: Common Ground," *New Options*, no. 22. Washington, DC: New Options, Inc., 1985.

Nikhilananda, Swami. *The Bhagavad Gita*. 1944. Reprint. New York: Ramakrishna-Vivekananda Center, 1969.

Pruitt, D. G. "Achieving Integrative Agreements in Negotiation." In M. H. Bazerman and R. J. Lewicki, eds., *Negotiating in Organizations*. Beverly Hills, CA: Sage, 1983.

Tansley, D. V. *Chakras — Rays and Radionics*. Essex, England: The C. W. Daniel Company Limited, 1984.

Thera, N. *The Heart of Buddhist Meditation*. 1962. Reprint. York Beach, ME: Samuel Weiser, Inc., 1973.

Vivekananda, Swami. *The Yogas and Other Works*. New York: Ramakrishna-Vivekananda Center, 1953.

Wood, E. *The Seven Rays*. 1925. Reprint. Wheaton, IL: Theosophical Publishing House, 1984.

Yogananda, P. *Autobiography of a Yogi*. 1946. Reprint. Los Angeles: Self-Realization Fellowship, 1969.